The Little
SEED

JESSE SUAREZ

ISBN 979-8-9907364-0-5 (paperback)
ISBN 979-8-9907364-1-2 (digital)

www.jessesplace.org

Unless otherwise indicated, all Scripture quotations are taken from the King James Version of the Holy Bible in the public domain.

Scripture is taken from the New King James Version. Copyright © 1982 by Thomas Nelson, Inc. Used by permission. All rights reserved.

Printed in the United States of America

To all the men, women, and children who have always believed that God created them for much more. To God be the glory, in Jesus's mighty name!

Open your mouth for the speechless, in the cause of all who are appointed to die. Open your mouth, judge righteously, and plead the cause of the poor and needy. (Proverbs 31:8–9 NKJV)

TABLE OF CONTENTS

IN THE BEGINNING, THERE WAS VISION

In the beginning God created the heaven and the earth. And the earth
was without form, and void; and darkness was upon the face of the
deep. And the Spirit of God moved upon the face of the waters. And
God said, Let there be light: and there was light.

—Genesis 1:1–3

This is talking about the beginning of creation, not the beginning of
everything. God resides in the realm of eternity, where there is no beginning and no end. We also know that "God is a Spirit" (John 4:24).

Then God said, "Let there be light," and there was light. He spoke
it, and it was so. However, before God spoke, from the spirit realm,
scripture tells us that "He beheld" the earth, which means that He in-
tently looked upon it. He beheld it, pondered it, and envisioned it by using the faculties of His imagination. God used His creativity! He didn't
speak concerning the facts of its current state (for just as real was the
reality of its hidden destiny), but He spoke to what it could be, to the
potential of what it could become. Earth, life, a paradise!

I beheld the earth, and, lo, it was without form and void;
and the heavens, and they had no light. (Jeremiah 4:23)

1

Everything was created by and for Jesus Christ. The Holy Bible teaches us that He created everything visible and invisible.

Here, *him* is referring to Christ:

> Who is the image of the invisible God, the firstborn of every creature: for by **him** were all things created that are in heaven, and that are in earth, visible and invisible, whether they be thrones, or dominions, or principalities, or powers: all things were created by **him**, and for **him**: and he is before all things, and by **him** all things consist. (Colossians 1:15–17, emphasis added)

The scripture says that by Jesus, all things were created that are in heaven and that are on earth. And "through faith we understand that the worlds were framed by the word of God, so that things which are seen were not made of things which do appear" (Hebrews 11:3). The things which are seen, the material and physical, came from the unseen, the invisible and spiritual. What is seen came forth from the heavenly places! (There's the seen, and then there's the unseen.)

What do we know about the heavenly places? We know that this is where Jesus is, and not only that, but this is the place that houses every imaginable and unimaginable blessing that has ever been bestowed upon us.

It is written,

> Blessed be the God and Father of our Lord Jesus Christ, who has blessed us with every spiritual blessing in the heavenly places in Christ. (Ephesians 1:3 NKJV)

"Has blessed us," as in the past tense, so it's something that has already been done. I can picture a heavenly warehouse with billions upon billions of shelves with an unlimited surplus of blessings! We are talking about the best of the good and fine things of God. This is coming from a

2

place where moth and rust do not destroy and where the streets are made of pure gold!

That's all good, but how do I get those blessings from over there to over here? How do I get it from heaven to earth? I don't need my blessings stored up, collecting dust on a spiritual shelf. There's pandemic and inflation down here, and in some places even famine, along with fear and sickness; there are also "wars and rumours of wars" (Matthew 24:6). We need the blessings so that we may put food on the table, put a roof over our heads, and further the kingdom of God.

How? Well, it first begins with having the knowledge that you're already qualified—the knowledge of what is already yours. Of having knowledge of what is already yours, by divine right!

When I was growing up, there was a saying that went, "And knowing is half the battle."

God's Word tells us,

> My people are destroyed for lack of knowledge.
> (Hosea 4:6)

Without the correct knowledge, our dreams will perish, our visions will perish, and even our legacies will perish. We will never get them off the ground. It's not our fault if we don't "know," for how can we know what we don't know? Everyone is unaware of this or that, at one point or another. However, after reading this book, you shall be without excuse for two things. One is the knowledge of how "you" can never perish but have everlasting life in Christ Jesus. And second, you'll have the knowledge of how you can make your every vision a reality and how you can see it come to pass!

My brothers and sisters, you are going to learn how to be who the Word says that you are already, how to have what the Word says belongs to you already, and how to do the impossible and miraculous works that the Word says that you can do already. And it all starts with having knowledge of Him—of Who God is.

Grace and peace be multiplied unto you through the **knowledge** of God, and of Jesus our Lord, according as his divine power hath given unto us all things that pertain unto life and godliness, through the **knowledge** of him that hath called us to glory and virtue: whereby are given unto us exceeding great and precious promises: that by these ye might be partakers of the divine nature, having escaped the corruption that is in the world through lust. (2 Peter 1:2–4, emphasis added)

Through this scripture, we learned that "His divine power has given to us [already] all things that pertain to life and godliness," through the knowledge of Him. For in Him, we are told of precious promises and precious blessings, even that we may be partakers of Jesus's divine nature while here on earth. Wow! Did the Scripture just tell us that? Yes, it did, and see, now you know that it is possible. What does that look like? It's hard to visualize it, right? That's why we need God to open up our spiritual eyes through His Word and His Spirit.

That the God of our Lord Jesus Christ, the Father of glory, may give unto you the spirit of wisdom and revelation in the **knowledge** of him: the eyes of your understanding being enlightened; that ye may know what is the hope of his calling, and what the riches of the glory of his inheritance in the saints. (Ephesians 1:17–18, emphasis added)

Again, we see that it's in the knowledge of Him. We are also told that "the eyes of our understanding" need to be enlightened so that we may know what our expectation is as children of God. So that we may know "what the riches of the glory of His inheritance in the saints" are. An inheritance that we have access to—in the here and now.

What does the "eyes of our understanding" mean? Well, the word *understanding* here translates into "***dianoia***" in Greek. This specific word also translates into *imagination* in the Gospel of Luke 1:51. This is a word that means "deep thought."

There are certain things in the Holy Bible and in life that we are only going to see and cause to be made manifest through the use of the deep thought of our imagination. God used it as He beheld (in deep thought) the earth, and then He created. He didn't use His deep thought because it was a complicated task, but because He took delight in His creation. He took His time—seven days—in which He used His creativity! (I can see Him smiling on the day of rest.) And we, having been created in His image and in His likeness (Genesis 1:26), are going to use it as well, as we fashion our lives after and upon "all the things that pertain to life and godliness" that He has already freely given to us.

So the knowledge is that He has already given us all things, but they are currently in the heavenly places. This knowledge of where our blessings are is good to have; it's like possessing a treasure map, but we want to go further. We want to hold them, feel them, and enjoy them. Trust me, our Heavenly Father also wants us to prosper and thrive, as His Word says,

> Beloved, I pray that you may prosper in all things and be
> in health, just as your soul prospers. (3 John 1:2 NKJV)

But as first it is the unseen, then it is the seen, so we, too, prosper in our soul and then in the outward person. (As our spirit man grows, all things subsequently fall into place.) We are made up of spirit, soul, and body (1 Thessalonians 5:23). We also know that as we think, we, in turn, do; that's the "will." And as we think, we also feel; that's the "emotions." So our soul (which is comprised of mind, will, and emotions) prospers as we renew our minds. This is a new mind that will be receptive and compatible with obeying and performing the Word and will of God.

I beseech you therefore, brethren, by the mercies of God, that ye present your bodies a living sacrifice, holy, acceptable unto God, which is your reasonable service. And be not conformed to this world: but be ye transformed by the renewing of your mind, that ye may prove what is that good, and acceptable, and perfect, will of God. (Romans 12:1–2)

We are transformed outwardly by the renewing of our minds inwardly. Thus, our mind is renewed through daily reading, meditating, and the application of His Word. Our minds are renewed through the use of "deep thought" in our imagination!

Everything in the Holy Bible was written for you so that you might receive knowledge of Him, of Who He is, and of everything that He can do in your life as your Heavenly Father. The Word opens your eyes.

Jesus Christ is still healing and giving sight to the blind. As the song goes, "Open the eyes of my heart, Lord. Open the eyes of my heart, I want to see You."

For whatsoever things were written aforetime were written for our learning, that we through patience and comfort of the scriptures might have hope. (Romans 15:4)

The Scriptures give us hope (**h**elps **o**urselves **p**lant **e**ndlessly), and our hope is a big thing because our hope is in Christ, through His Word, and there's nothing bigger than that. Many of us can relate to or remember how our lives were empty and hopeless when we were without God. We had no knowledge of Him, and when that's the case, "anything goes," and in one way or another, we, as a people, were being destroyed. And it didn't matter. We were merely existing, but we were not living, at least not the "life and life more abundant" that Jesus came to give us (John 10:10).

Where there is no vision, the people perish.
(Proverbs 29:18)

In the Hebrew language, the word vision here speaks of a "prophetic vision" or a revelatory vision. As in a Word from God, it's a revelation-illumination of His Word. When God personally speaks to you through a prophetic vision, it changes everything. You begin to care and have a sense of direction; it births hope!

Behold, get ready because God, the creator of the universe, is going to speak to you through the following chapters. For assuredly, I say to you that if you apply the spiritual principles held herein, your life will never be the same.

Are you ready?

Let's go!

IN THE BEGINNING, THERE WAS VISION

Then the LORD answered me and said: "Write the vision and make it plain on tablets, that he may run who reads it."

—Habakkuk 2:2 NKJV

_____

THE PROPHETIC VISION

In the beginning was the Word, and the Word
was with God, and the Word was God.

—John 1:1

"The Word of God" is one of Jesus's names (Revelation 19:13). The *Word* is a common name used when referring to Jesus. Another name for Jesus, which is not as commonly used, is "the Seed," with a capital *S*. We see this reference in the book of Galatians:

> Now to Abraham and his Seed were the promises made.
> He does not say, "And to seeds," as of many, but as of
> one, "And to your Seed," who is Christ. (Galatians 3:16
> NKJV)

So now let's go back and see the scripture in John 1:1 through a different lens (different name) for a moment so that we may gain a deeper understanding. "In the beginning was the Seed, and the Seed was with God, and the Seed was God." Also, where it reads, "And the Word was made flesh" (John 1:14), we now see, "And the Seed became flesh." Jesus taught us that "the seed is the word of God" (Luke 8:11).

We can see that in the beginning (in eternity, in the heavenly places) was the Son, the Word, the Seed, and then the Son, the Word, the Seed became flesh. He came to pass. He became incarnate. The once-spiritual form in heaven became a bodily form on earth. The invisible became visible. Jesus really and literally came down from heaven (John 3:13). The apostle John bears witness by giving personal testimony, saying,

> That which was from the beginning, which we have heard, which we have seen with our eyes, which we have looked upon, and our hands have handled, of the Word of life; (For the life was manifested, and we have seen it, and bear witness, and shew unto you that eternal life, which was with the Father, and was manifested unto us;) that which we have seen and heard declare we unto you, that ye also may have fellowship with us: and truly our fellowship is with the Father, and with his Son Jesus Christ. (1 John 1:1–3)

How do we know that God wants us "tinkering" and siphoning down things from heaven unto earth? Because it's His will; we are even instructed of this in the Lord's Prayer.

> After this manner therefore pray ye: Our Father which art in heaven, Hallowed be thy name. Thy kingdom come, Thy will be done in earth, as it is in heaven. (Matthew 6:9–10)

Whatever we loose (set at liberty by declaring Scripture) on earth will be loosed, released, and discharged in heaven.

This is Jesus speaking,

> Verily I say unto you, Whatsoever ye shall bind on earth shall be bound in heaven: and whatsoever ye shall loose on earth shall be loosed in heaven. (Matthew 18:18)

Then how did Jesus do it? How was He transferred, teleported, and manifested? First, the Son was beheld in the bosom of the Father (John 1:18). And then God spoke it! The first prophecy ever given was made in the garden of Eden, and it was concerning "the Seed," Jesus Christ. The prophecy was about how the Seed of a woman would one day crush the head of the snake, Satan.

> And I will put enmity between you and the woman, and between your seed and her Seed; He shall bruise your head, and you shall bruise His heel. (Genesis 3:15 NKJV)

The Holy Bible shows us that one of the first things that happened was that while the Seed was still in heaven, He was being spoken of down here on earth. Prophecy is not prophecy unless man knows about it, for it is God Who gives prophecy to His children and the world. "Surely the Lord God will do nothing, but he revealeth his secret unto his servants the prophets" (Amos 3:7).

The prophet Isaiah wrote,

> I have declared the former things from the beginning; and they went forth out of my mouth, and I shewed them; I did them suddenly, and they came to pass. I have even from the beginning declared it to thee; before it came to pass I shewed it thee: lest thou shouldest say, Mine idol hath done them, and my graven image, and my molten image, hath commanded them. (Isaiah 48:3 and 5)

God's Word resounds, saying,

> Remember the former things of old: for I am God, and
> there is none else; I am God, and there is none like me,
> declaring the end from the beginning, and from ancient
> times the things that are not yet done, saying, My coun-
> sel shall stand, and I will do all my pleasure. (Isaiah
> 46:9–10)

Only God can declare a prophecy like this because He knows it all. He is the alpha and the omega, the beginning and the end. So when His Word comes to pass, He and only He gets all the glory!

> Behold, the former things are come to pass, and new
> things do I declare: before they spring forth I tell you
> of them. (Isaiah 42:9)

God has something to declare to this generation. The book of Isaiah tells us about a prisoner who wants to be freed. He doesn't want to die behind bars, and he doesn't want to run out of food. But God reminds him of how He released over one million captives (from Egyptian bondage) in one day and opened for them the Red Sea, which they walked through as if on dry land. And God didn't mention it, but we all know that while they wandered about in the wilderness for forty years, they never ran out of food, for the Lord caused it to rain down manna from heaven (Exodus 16:35). There has always been a plan. He does not say, "Seek ye me in vain" (Isaiah 45:19). God has used this wilderness experience to hide His Word in our hearts. For what purpose? I mean, what could a prisoner of **hope** possibly accomplish for himself, let alone others?

> The captive exhile hasteneth that he may be loosed,
> and that he should not die in the pit, nor that his bread
> should fail. But I am the LORD thy God, that divided
> the sea, whose waves roared: The LORD of hosts is
> his name. And I have put my words in thy mouth, and I
> have covered thee in the shadow of mine hand, **that I**
> **may plant the heavens**, and lay the foundations of the
> earth, and say unto Zion, Thou art my people. (Isaiah
> 51:14–16, emphasis added)

It's natural to look around and focus on all the wrong things when you are in a pit; however, nothing good will come out of that. God wants us to latch on to Him through His Word, His visions, and His prophecies. He wants us to look up. "I will lift up mine eyes unto the hills, from whence cometh my help" (Psalm 121:1). Our help comes from the Lord.

There's a purpose for the tragedy that has transpired, and the reason is that God wants to "plant the heavens" through our mouths. That prisoner whom the prophet Isaiah wrote about is "me!" The captive is "a people," as in many. So will you declare in faith that it's you too?

Use us, Lord.

> Behold, I and the children whom the LORD hath giv-
> en me are for signs and for wonders in Israel from the
> LORD of hosts, which dwelleth in mount Zion. (Isaiah
> 8:18)

How are the heavens planted? They are planted through the Word of God. You must first find a specific scripture (which is a seed), a promise, or a prophecy. His Word is in heaven, standing firm, waiting to take effect in our lives. The Word is for us. The psalmist declared,

> For ever, O LORD, thy word is settled in heaven.
> (Psalm 119:89)

You can ask God concerning anything and see if He doesn't download upon you a response by sending you a spiritual email with the answer, the remedy, and the solution!

> He sendeth forth his commandment upon the earth: his
> word runneth very swiftly. (Psalm 147:15)

The Word is established (standing still) in heaven, but it has to be moved, commanded, and directed. Within your heart, you hold the control to bind and release, and you can use it to cause blessings to rain down from heaven.

> Thus saith the LORD, the Holy One of Israel, and his
> Maker, Ask me of things to come concerning my sons,
> and concerning the work of my hands command ye me.
> (Isaiah 45:11)

It is only through the Holy Bible that we are able to know what's in heaven. And again, for I cannot emphasize enough that "the Word was created for 'us,'" and though it is established in heaven, down here on earth, His Word is a lamp unto my feet and a light unto my path (Psalm 119:105). Man is just incapable of properly maneuvering through life without it.

The following scripture helps us better understand how the Word operates. The Word of God is a seed through which everything on earth happens.

> Being born again, not of corruptible seed, but of incor-
> ruptible, by the word of God, which liveth and abideth
> for ever. For all flesh is as grass, and all the glory of
> man as the flower of grass. The grass withereth, and the
> flower thereof falleth away: but the word of the Lord

> endureth for ever. And this is the word which by the
> gospel is preached unto you. (1 Peter 1:23–25)

Give this deep thought: If you can be born again and "become a new creature" (2 Corinthians 5:17), a new creation through the incorruptible seed, then anything and everything is possible through the same Word.

We just read, "But the word of the Lord endureth for ever. And this is the word which by the gospel is preached unto you." This is telling us that the Word that is established in heaven forever and the gospel, the Holy Bible that we hold in our hands, are one and the same. It means that the Word does not change, and the Scriptures that we hold are proof positive of what is established in heaven and of what can be ours. It can be likened to holding a receipt, which is why it gives us so much hope. And because the receipt is given to us by a living God, it is a living hope.

> God is not a man, that he should lie; neither the son of
> man, that he should repent: hath he said, and shall he
> not do it? or hath he spoken, and shall he not make it
> good? (Numbers 23:19)

Joshua, the son of Nun, before dying, in essence, said to his people, "This I know about God, and so do you, that if He says something, then He'll do it." Imagine being in that congregation and hearing Joshua speak and knowing that what he is saying is true.

> And, behold, this day I am going the way of all the earth:
> and ye know **in all your hearts** and **in all your souls**,
> that not one thing hath failed of all the good things
> which the LORD your God spake concerning you; all
> are come to pass unto you, and not one thing hath failed
> thereof. (Joshua 23:14, emphasis added)

15

By now, you are probably wondering, "Where is the Seed (the Word of God) to be planted?" right? Jesus will answer this for us, as He also taught His disciples in the parable of the soils, saying,

> And he said unto them, Know ye not this parable? And how then will ye know all parables? The sower soweth the word. And these are they by the way side, where the word is sown; but when they have heard, Satan cometh immediately, and taketh away **the word that was sown in their hearts**. (Mark 4:13–15, emphasis added)

"Know ye not this parable?" is the same as saying, "Do you not understand this parable?" The main point that Jesus wants us to understand is that the Word of God is sown in our hearts. This is the key that unlocks the whole thing of knowing and understanding the functions of His Word. The mechanics are the same as those of a seed being planted (sown); it's that simple. God wants us to understand His Word because, if we don't, it becomes unfruitful to us. There is more to it than just reading it; it is a heart thing. For not all who see really see, and not all who hear really hear, as Jesus repeated the words of the prophet who prophesied:

> And in them is fulfilled the prophecy of Esaias, which saith, By hearing ye shall hear, and shall not understand; and seeing ye shall see, and shall not perceive: for this people's heart is waxed gross, and their ears are dull of hearing, and their eyes they have closed; lest at any time they should see with their eyes and hear with their ears, and should understand with their heart, and should be converted, and I should heal them. (Matthew 13:14–15)

When we don't understand what we see or hear in the Word with our hearts, the devil comes and snatches it away. It gets stolen.

> When any one heareth the word of the kingdom, and understandeth it not, then cometh the wicked one, and catcheth away that which was sown in his heart. This is he which received seed by the way side. (Matthew 13:19)

However, those who have the eyes of their understanding enlightened are those to whom Jesus said,

> But blessed are your eyes, for they see: and your ears, for they hear. For verily I say unto you, That many prophets and righteous men have desired to see those things which ye see, and have not seen them; and to hear those things which ye hear, and have not heard them. (Matthew 13:16–17)

And Jesus further presents the benefits of using the "deep thought" (*dianoia*), "imagination" of our heart.

> But he that received seed into the good ground is he that heareth the word, and understandeth it; which also beareth fruit, and bringeth forth, some an hundredfold, some sixty, some thirty. (Matthew 13:23)

There you have it. "What God's heavenly Word says about you is sown inward, the invisible." And it bears fruit outward, "Revealed, prophecy fulfilled"—the visible!

When God spoke prophecy in the garden of Eden, that Word became anchored in the heart of man. And heaven was now able to take

17

residence in Adam's and Eve's hearts in seed form. The heart is not only a point of contact with heaven but also a point of delivery!

In the following chapter, we will see the process of how Jesus went from being the Seed to full maturity from beginning to end.

THE PROPHETIC VISION

Then the LORD answered me and said: "Write the vision and make it plain on tablets, that he may run who reads it."

—Habakkuk 2:2 NKJV

_____
_____
_____
_____
_____
_____
_____
_____
_____
_____
_____
_____
_____
_____
_____
_____
_____
_____
_____
_____
_____
_____
_____
_____

CHAPTER 3

THE PROCESS OF THE VISION

So, it remains, for the rest of mankind, that the only wall between the "visible and invisible" seems to be the one of ignorance. For Jesus Christ tore the veil, the wall of separation, as He cried out in a loud voice, "It is finished!" (Matthew 27:50–51; John 19:30), when He gave up His Spirit on the cross. ("Now all things can be yours. Now you can have full access.")

The heavens declare, "Worthy is the Lamb that was slain to receive power, and riches, and wisdom, and strength, and honour, and glory, and blessing" (Revelation 5:12). Do you think that Jesus needed or wanted any of those things? Absolutely not. He was crucified so that He could give them to us. As it is written, "He that spared not his own Son, but delivered him up for us all, how shall he not with him also freely give us all things?" (Romans 8:32).

Now let's revisit the scripture again:

> Grace and peace be multiplied unto you through the **knowledge** of God, and of Jesus our Lord, according as his divine power hath given unto us all things that pertain unto life and godliness, through the **knowledge** of him that hath called us to glory and virtue: whereby are given unto us exceeding great and precious promises:

that by these ye might be partakers of the divine nature, having escaped the corruption that is in the world
through lust. (2 Peter 1:2–4, emphasis added)

A person reads and says, "Amazing, wonderful, how encouraging!" "What blessings, promises, and riches!" "Prophecies and revelations!" They can even shed tears and get the chills. But once they close
the Book, the Life and power remain imprinted on the page, and because
it never left, it never got transferred, and therefore, they don't become
"partakers." You, on the other hand, when you read the Word of God,
you can receive it because you understand that "every spiritual blessing
is already yours, and if you want it to become converted into a tangible
blessing that you can personally hold, all that you have to do is to plant
it in your heart." In other words, you know "what to do with it," and
you know how to handle the seed of God. You have the knowledge that
"if you want to be fruitful, you must first be plantful (seedful)." It's this
understanding that makes the difference and will set you apart.

The results in your life will be so evident that this time next season,
both friend and foe shall exclaim,"Wow! What happened to you?"

"Jesus happened!" "But how?"

"The sower sows the Word."

"In English, tell us in English."

"Okay, this spiritual truth can be likened to downloading an app
on a smartphone. You can hold a smartphone in your hand, visit the
App Store, and then personally view all the different apps and even read
about the particular jobs that they perform. Different apps provide different services. But for you to enjoy all the benefits and functions of the
app, you 'must' first download it onto the hardware of your smartphone
or computer device. The apps were designed to only operate in this manner; there's just no other way around it. In the same way, the Seed of
God must first be downloaded unto our hearts for it to be effective and
for us to reap its benefits."

You know what they say: "If the APPles 'of our vision' ain't becoming, growing, or showing, it's because we ain't downloading."

It's time to get into the process. Let's do some downloading!

> And no man hath ascended up to heaven, but he that came **down** from heaven, even the Son of man which is in heaven. (John 3:13, emphasis added)

The Holy Bible gives us a detailed process and record of how Jesus, the Son of Man, came **down** from heaven. We also already settled and established that one of Jesus's names is the Seed.

In the beginning, the Seed was in heaven, the spirit realm of eternity. That's where everything comes from for the believer. This is the foundation and the starting point.

> But thou, Bethlehem Ephratah, though thou be little among the thousands of Judah, yet out of thee shall he come forth unto me that is to be ruler in Israel; whose goings forth have been from of old, from **everlasting**. (Micah 5:2, emphasis added)

Secondly, prophecy was given by the LORD in the garden of Eden, declaring that the Messiah was to come to earth by way of a Seed (Genesis 3:15). Prophecy was "spoken" concerning the Seed, Who was currently in heaven.

Then all throughout the ages, the prophets of old wrote and spoke what they heard and saw from God concerning the Seed that was to come.

These are just a few of the many prophecies recorded:

- The Scepter. "I shall see him, but not now" (Numbers 24:17).
- The Son. "Behold, a virgin shall conceive" (Isaiah 7:14).
- The Mighty God. "For unto us a child is born" (Isaiah 9:6).

- The Messiah. "Messiah the Prince" (Daniel 9:25).
- The King. "[Cometh] lowly riding upon a [donkey]" (Zechariah 9:9).
- Jesus! "They pierced his side" (Zechariah 12:10).
- Jesus! "He was resurrected" (Psalm 16:10 and 49:15).
- Jesus! "He ascended to heaven" (Psalm 68:18).

By prophesying, they were sowing seed. (You have to sow it before you grow it.)

After the Seed of God had been written, spoken of, and broadcasted—both near and abroad, "the fulness of the time was come" (Galatians 4:4), where He needed to be conceived in the heart of a believing host. The Greek word for *seed* is "***sperma***" (Galatians 3:16), from which we get today's word for *sperm*. Thus, the Word of God is the *sperma* of God.

The *sperma* of God can only reproduce through the heart of a believer.

> And in the sixth month the angel Gabriel was sent from God unto a city of Galilee, named Nazareth, to a virgin espoused to a man whose name was Joseph, of the house of David; and the virgin's name was Mary. And the angel came in unto her, and said, Hail, thou that art highly favoured, the Lord is with thee: blessed art thou among women. And when she saw him, she was troubled at his saying, and cast in her mind what manner of salutation this should be. And the angel said unto her, Fear not, Mary: for thou hast found favour with God. And, behold, thou shalt conceive in thy womb, and bring forth a son, and shalt call his name JESUS. He shall be great, and shall be called the Son of the Highest: and the Lord God shall give unto him the throne of his father David: and he shall reign over the house of Jacob for ever;

and of his kingdom there shall be no end. Then said
Mary unto the angel, How shall this be, seeing I know
not a man? And the angel answered and said unto her,
The Holy Ghost shall come upon thee, and the power of
the Highest shall overshadow thee: therefore also that
holy thing which shall be born in thee shall be called the
Son of God. And, behold, thy cousin Elisabeth, she hath
also conceived a son in her old age: and this is the sixth
month with her, who was called barren. For with God
nothing shall be impossible. And Mary said, Behold the
handmaid of the Lord; **be it unto me according to thy
word**. And the angel departed from her. (Luke 1:26–38,
emphasis added)

The prophetic vision was presented to the virgin by the angel Gabriel. He was speaking in the future tense: "You will conceive," and "the Holy Spirit will come upon you." Though it hadn't happened yet, God already knew, for He knows the end from the beginning. However, Mary had free will, and at that moment, she had to make a decision. And the call of God upon her life was contingent on her response: "For many are called, but few are chosen" (Matthew 22:14).

For the Holy Spirit to impregnate the womb of Mary, she first had to have the Seed-Word implanted in the womb of her heart.

The next stage of the process was extremely critical. Mary confessed, and she was only able to confess because she wholeheartedly believed. Her testimony was so strong and convincing that her husband-to-be, Joseph, was ready to end the whole wedding (Matthew 1:18–20). She made a confession of her pregnancy without having any proof besides what had been revealed to her by the angel Gabriel from God. The vision is voice activated!

As we vocalize the vision, things start happening (confirmation). Mary took action and went to visit her cousin. Once there, Elizabeth became filled with the Holy Spirit and prophesied over her, saying,

> And blessed is she that believed: for there shall be a
> performance of those things which were told her from
> the Lord. (Luke 1:45)

Mary's belief would cause her to see a performance, fulfillment, and manifestation of what she had heard.

Then finally came the birth of Jesus, where the Seed was converted into the Son. The One in heaven, of Whom it was spoken about, could now finally be seen on earth, walking about.

> And she **brought forth** her firstborn son, and wrapped
> him in swaddling clothes, and laid him in a manger;
> because there was no room for them in the inn. (Luke
> 2:7, emphasis added)

Think about the many kingdoms, empires, and nations! All the different movements, crusades, and organizations that have been brought forth using this method and spiritual principles.

A vision, a Word, or a revelation is received; it can even be a dream, a plan, or a kingdom idea, and it's then written down, mass broadcasted, confessed with the mouth, and believed in the heart. And action steps are taken to give it life. For faith without works is what? (dead)

There's a process to manifesting your visions here in the natural realm. After it is here, the entity begins to take on form; it grows as Christ also did, once He was born. When Jesus was eight days old, He was held and carried around in the temple by His parents and Simeon. He was also "spoken over" (prophesied to) by Simeon and by the prophetess Anna (Luke 2:21–38), and yes, women can be prophets!

That's how visions begin. We delicately hold them in our arms, nurturing them and speaking prophetically to them. Then they take off on their own, and they handle business as Jesus did, as we now see Him through the scriptures at twelve years old.

> And when he was twelve years old, they went up to
> Jerusalem after the custom of the feast. And when they
> had fulfilled the days, as they returned, the child Jesus
> tarried behind in Jerusalem; and Joseph and his mother
> knew not of it. But they, supposing him to have been
> in the company, went a day's journey; and they sought
> him among their kinsfolk and acquaintance. And when
> they found him not, they turned back again to Jerusa-
> lem, seeking him. And it came to pass, that after three
> days they found him in the temple, sitting in the midst
> of the doctors, both hearing them, and asking them
> questions. And all that heard him were astonished at his
> understanding and answers. And when they saw him,
> they were amazed: and his mother said unto him, Son,
> why hast thou thus dealt with us? behold, thy father and
> I have sought thee sorrowing. And he said unto them,
> How is it that ye sought me? wist ye not that I must be
> about my Father's business? (Luke 2:42–49)

The temple had remained the same, but Jesus hadn't. He had developed. In the same place where He had once been held and carried,
He now held them all in awe and amazement as He carried them in deep
dialogue. The One Who was once spoken over was now speaking forth.
It didn't happen overnight, though; twelve years had elapsed. It was a
process, which went as follows:

> And Jesus increased in wisdom and stature, and in fa-
> vour with God and man. (Luke 2:52)

What helps us to grow, to increase, and to be productive?
Be the vision: Jesus and His message were one. The vision must be
lived out, thus, making your life a living and embodied advertisement.
Jesus said,

27

Think not that I am come to destroy the law, or the
prophets: I am not come to destroy, but fulfil. (Matthew
5:17)

Build a team: Nothing big or of worth or value ever gets done by
just one person. A team is always needed. Even our Master Jesus Christ
made use of this principle. To build a team, recruiting and training are
necessary.

Recruitment,

- "And he saith unto them, Follow me, and I will make you
  fishers of men" (Matthew 4:19).
- "And as Jesus passed forth from thence, he saw a man,
  named Matthew, sitting at the receipt of custom: and he
  saith unto him, Follow me. And he arose, and followed him"
  (Matthew 9:9).
- "And when he had called unto him his twelve disciples,
  he gave them power against unclean spirits, to cast them
  out, and to heal all manner of sickness and all manner of disease"
  (Matthew 10:1).

As the twelve recruits saw Jesus in action, they were "picking up
game," seeing firsthand how it's done. "And it came to pass afterward,
that he went throughout every city and village, preaching and shewing
the glad tidings of the kingdom of God: and the twelve were with him"
(Luke 8:1).

Delegate: After Jesus recruited His twelve disciples, He delegated
tasks to them. He sent them out on "missions" so that they could get
their feet wet. For the most part, the job will always be hands-on (life is
real, and the vision won't get done/accomplished by itself). They have
to leave the nest and spread their wings. Sometimes they will be successful, and other times they won't, but it's a learning process. It is being

out in the field that serves as their academy, and through their sweat and toil, they shall gain experience.

- "And Jesus rebuked the devil; and he departed out of him: and the child was cured from that very hour. Then came the disciples to Jesus apart, and said, Why could not we cast him out?" (Matthew 17:18–19).
- "After these things the Lord appointed other seventy also, and sent them two and two before his face into every city and place, whither he himself would come" (Luke 10:1).
- "And the seventy returned again with joy, saying, Lord, even the devils are subject unto us through thy name" (Luke 10:17).

Incorporate: Jesus incorporated the "apostles." He brought them "in," becoming one with them. It's one thing for a follower to believe in your vision; however, it's a totally different thing for them to become one with you. And the only way that this is made possible is through "LOVE." Love is what caused Jonathan's soul to become knitted together with King David's. "Jonathan loved him as his own soul" (1 Samuel 18:1). It was love that caused all of Israel to say to King David, "Behold, we are thy bone and thy flesh" (1 Chronicles 11:1).

Of love, Jesus said the following:

> Greater love hath no man than this, that a man lay down
> his life for his friends. (John 15:13)

We know that He loved His own who were in the world, and He loved them to the end (John 13:1). So we see that business is one thing, but love trumps *all*. Jesus embraced them and compared His relationship with them to that of the Father with Him. And then He prayed that they would be on the same footing as Him in relation to and as recipients of the Father's love, which is what Christ valued the most.

- "And the glory which thou gavest me I have given them; that they may be one, even as we are one: I in them, and thou in me, that they may be made perfect in one; and that the world may know that thou hast sent me, and hast loved them, as thou hast loved me" (John 17:22–23).
- "And I have declared unto them thy name, and will declare it: that the love wherewith thou hast loved me may be in them, and I in them" (John 17:26).
- "But above all these things put on love, which is the bond of perfection" (Colossians 3:14 NKJV).

"You've gotta love your crew," for God has entrusted them to your care. You are them, and they are you. Be one with them. Visions are brought about by people, and love is the perfect glue that will unite and hold your people together. "One alone is but a river. However, together we form a mighty ocean. A river can be controlled, an ocean cannot!"

So if you want your vision to have vigor, force, and movement, remember two things. One is Jesus, and the second is *love*.

Reproduction: A disciple is somebody who is training to be like Christ as they apply the scriptures. Jesus reproduced and reproduces Himself through the Word. We already know that the child of God is born again through the incorruptible Seed, which is the Word of God (1 Peter 1:23). Jesus also modeled the Word so that we could have His footsteps as an example to follow (John 13:15; 1 Peter 2:21). And it is the application of His Word that sets us apart, for it positions us on a whole different playing field. While in prayer, Jesus discloses,

I have given them thy word; and the world hath hated them, because they are not of the world, even as I am not of the world. (John 17:14)

Visualize a worldwide platoon of "out-of-this-world" Jesus followers marching to the sound of God's heartbeat. All are synchronized by the same Word, page, and Book! All of us are advancing with one accord.

One time, Jesus was teaching through the use of parables. The subject was the kingdom of heaven, and He used the illustration of grain to depict how it produces a crop despite the opposition of the tares. The disciples didn't quite understand, so He explained the meaning to them. Jesus's response was "kernel" and "keynote" to our questions, identity, and purpose here on earth.

> He answered and said unto them, He that soweth the
> good seed is the Son of man; the field is the world; the
> good seed are the children of the kingdom; but the tares
> are the children of the wicked one. (Matthew 13:37–38)

Do you recall those "Seed lenses" that we used earlier? Okay, put them on real quick, and let's view this scripture again. It now reads, "He who sows the good seed is the 'Seed.' The field is the world, the good seeds are the children of the kingdom...The Seed sows the seed." The good seeds are the children (or sons) of the kingdom; that's speaking of you and me. So the question is this, "If Jesus is the big Seed, then what does that make us?" (Yes, you are correct. We are **the little seeds**.") He has literally sown Himself in you, and you are now a seed that is ready to bear much fruit.

Though we were created in the image and likeness of God, we can still learn and get insight from the following scripture, especially since Jesus referred to us as seeds in His teachings:

> And God said, Let the earth bring forth grass, the herb
> yielding seed, and the fruit tree yielding fruit after his
> kind, whose seed is in itself, upon the earth: and it was
> so. (Genesis 1:11)

Because the incorruptible Seed is now in us (whose seed is in itself), we can now yield fruit according to His kind!

Give ear, for I tell you what may seem like a mystery but is yet no mystery at all. I tell you a grandiose truth that may be hard to accept if you don't receive it and behold it with your heart. And it is "that Christ Jesus came to earth to duplicate Himself in you" (He is growing in you, and as you "yield yourself to Him, He shall yield His fruits through you").

The Seed is the Word of God that not only fills us with hope but also works and serves like currency by which all transactions are made from heaven to earth. It's what operates the heavenly supply and demand, in that the more that it is planted, the more that it draws thereof. The supply is never-ending because the Word is never-ending. That's why, in Christ, we have abundance; we have more than enough.

In the Old Testament, when the children of Israel cried out to the LORD in their troubles and distresses as they wandered through the wilderness, "He sent his word, and healed them, and delivered them from their destructions" (Psalm 107:20). In like manner, He has also sent His Word to bless us, comfort us, and protect us. And most importantly, He sent His Word to reproduce Himself in us! Jesus Christ is our destiny.

Jesus poured Himself into His followers, infusing them with His vision, His spirit (of quality and manner), and His teachings. Most significantly, He imparted upon them what He had told the Father in prayer: "I have given them Your Word."

We are not duplicating ourselves. We are working in tandem (together) with God, and it is Jesus Who is the One being reproduced. Therefore, our vision should serve as a platform and an incubator that spawns a conducive environment through which we and our followers can push the "Jesus" agenda. Remember, it's all about Jesus; we just get blessed in the process.

If we emulate His pattern, He will emanate His love and power through our lives and echo through this generation and the ones to come.

Send them out: Jesus commissioned His offspring, saying, "Go ye therefore, and teach [make disciples of] all nations, baptizing them in the name of the Father, and of the Son, and of the Holy Ghost: teaching them to observe all things whatsoever I have commanded you: and, lo, I am with you always, even unto the end of the world. Amen" (Matthew 28:19–20).

- "And he said unto them, Go ye into all the world, and preach the gospel to every creature" (Mark 16:15).
- "Then said Jesus to them again, Peace be unto you: as my Father hath sent me, even so send I you" (John 20:21).
- "The disciple is not above his master: but everyone that is perfect [perfectly trained and mature] shall be as his master" (Luke 6:40).

Their mission was to teach others (the new recruits, the little seeds) to observe, obey, and follow by putting into practice all the things that they themselves had been taught and seen modeled by Jesus Christ. The cycle would then repeat itself and start all over again, this time with them as the leaders and teachers.

Let's not try to reinvent the wheel. We need to "stick to the Script." The system is foolproof; it has been successfully working for over two thousand years, ever since Jesus set it in place.

"And, lo, I am with you always, even to the end of the world." When Jesus sent them out, He remained in contact with them through His Spirit to encourage them by making them "remember" and also so that He could continue to teach them.

- "But the Comforter, which is the Holy Ghost, whom the Father will send in my name, he shall teach you all things, and bring all things to your remembrance, whatsoever I have said unto you" (John 14:26).

We must keep in contact with "our people" as we send them out to start a new base. They are our eyes, our ears, and our mouth; they are our hands and our feet. (They are the arteries to our vision.) Now we can be in many places at the same time. They will also only go as far and do as much as the training that they are given, so make sure to give them everything that you have. The class sessions are never over, so you must continue growing yourself so that you may continue feeding and building them.

That's how the Seed came down from heaven, and that's how Jesus did it. This is God's method. Now go and apply it to your vision!

THE PROCESS OF THE VISION

Then the LORD answered me and said: "Write the vision and make it plain on tablets, that he may run who reads it."

—Habakkuk 2:2 NKJV

_____

_____

_____

_____

_____

_____

_____

_____

_____

_____

_____

_____

_____

_____

_____

_____

_____

_____

_____

_____

_____

_____

_____

CHAPTER 4

THE VISION OF HABAKKUK

As the following scriptures in this teaching shall reveal, your vision may be more prophetic than what you have formally realized. "For the testimony of Jesus is the spirit of prophecy" (Revelation 19:10). In other words, whatever testifies of Jesus Christ inherently has a "prophetic element." It carries that "catchy" nature with it, for Jesus is not only the link between us and our vision, but He is also the link to all things—seen and unseen, whether in the past, in the present, or in the future. In Him, all things are linked together. Jesus "is" the linchpin! He is more than just data. He's also the motherboard and the electrical current running the whole show. Jesus is "upholding all things by the word of his power" (Hebrews 1:3). "And he is before all things, and by him all things consist" (Colossians 1:17). Jesus Christ is the God particle that modern science refuses to admit that "He" is!

Your <u>documented</u> vision is <u>evidence</u> that can be analyzed to verify if it gives testimony to Jesus Christ. It is evidence because it is physically on paper, in written form (or in whatever form or medium it has been caught or held in). It is a document, and because its outcome shall point to Christ, it already testifies of Him (as Levi, who would be born later in time, paid tithes through Abraham, so to speak, for he was still in the loins of his father when Melchizedek met him (Hebrews 7:8–10).), and if it is "the testimony of Jesus," it has the…? (You got it! The spirit of prophecy.)

In the same way that "the Spirit itself beareth witness with our spirit, that we are children of God" (Romans 8:16), the Spirit also bears witness, "validating" to our spirit and to the spirit of others that our visions are of Him through the spirit of prophecy and confirmed by the Word.

Here are three principles to know about God:

- "He cannot deny himself" (2 Timothy 2:13). He has to testify.
- "God also bearing them witness, both with signs and wonders, and with divers miracles, and gifts of the Holy Ghost, according to his own will" (Hebrews 2:4). He testifies through His children with miracles and different gifts of the Holy Spirit.
- "Him who worketh all things after the counsel of his own will" (Ephesians 1:11). This includes your works when they testify of Him.

These principles can be applied to your vision. They get Him involved.

"To catch the vision" is to capture its prophetic spirit that points to that which is not here yet. How does one do that? "How does one catch a vision from God?" The Holy Bible has a lot to say in regard to this subject. God personally spoke the first prophecy in the garden of Eden, and then throughout the ages, He continued to speak prophecies through the mouths of His prophets. This process was captured and laid down, and its amazing details are clearly seen in the book of Habakkuk. We are now going to learn how a vision is set up.

> I will stand upon my watch, and set me upon the tower, and will watch to see what he will say unto me, and what I shall answer when I am reproved. And the LORD answered me, and said, Write the vision, and make it plain upon tables [tablets], that he may run that readeth it. For the vision is yet for an appointed time, but at the end it shall speak, and not lie: though it tarry, wait for

it; because it will surely come, it will not tarry. Behold,
his soul which is lifted up is not upright in him: but the
just shall live by his faith. (Habakkuk 2:1–4)

The prophet Habakkuk was instructed by God to write the vision. But as we shall be enlightened, when it comes to visions, writing can be a broad term. The prophet began by saying to himself, "I will stand my watch and set myself upon the tower." He positioned himself, which has to do with posture. He placed himself in a position to receive from God. The tower was the high wall that surrounded a city (he was a watchman). Habakkuk also said, "I will watch to see what He will say unto me." This man made his preparation by consciously separating himself and making arrangements to hear from God.

At times, the best way to go high is to go low. "Humble yourselves therefore under the mighty hand of God, that he may exalt you in due time" (1 Peter 5:6). You can bow your head, bend your knees, or lay prostrate flat on the floor. There's no right or wrong way. Just make sure that you "seek Him with all your heart"; this guarantees that you will find Him (Jeremiah 29:13–14). Give Him your time with a humble heart, and it will be of the highest quality.

We are also able to take notice of the concrete conviction of the prophet. He said to himself, "I will watch and see what He will say unto me." And He did! "And the LORD answered me." He had the assurance that God would speak to him. When God speaks to you, it can be the smallest still voice ever, but it'll have so much power that "you won't be able to shut up about it." It's like putting jet fuel in the gas tank of a moped. For instance, the LORD gave me the title for this book. He spoke it audibly in my heart, and nobody had to tell me, within seconds, I had caught it (written it), translated it, transmuted it, and transferred it to paper! Everybody with whom I came into contact heard the story. I was frenzied! I had called my mom from the prison phone, and I gave her a whole sermon in two minutes—all in one breath! I ended by prophesying, tearing up, and having a cracking voice because I was so overwhelmed by the Holy Spirit. I said, "You'll see. You'll see. One day, people are going to say, 'You're the mother of the guy who wrote *The Little Seed?*'" When you know that something is from God, you are completely sold out to it, and nothing can convince you or persuade you otherwise.

Habakkuk was instructed to "write the vision, and make it plain upon tables, that he may run that readeth it" (Habakkuk 2:2). The focus momentarily shifted to the runner. In the Old Testament (and in the New Testament), the runners were used to dispense and distribute information or messages. This is how information was communicated and distributed before television, radio, cell phones, and social media.

> Then said Ahimaaz the son of Zadok, Let me now run, and bear the king tidings, how that the LORD hath avenged him of his enemies. (2 Samuel 18:19)

The runner ran with the news. Sometimes it was good, and other times it wasn't. His job was to get it there—to deliver it. The watchman would set himself high on the lookout for incoming news.

> And David sat between the two gates: and the watchman went up to the roof over the gate unto the wall, and lifted his eyes, and looked, and behold a man running alone. (2 Samuel 18:24)

Though there's a distinction between the watchman and the runner, at times the prophet was both, as was the case with the prophet Elijah (1 Kings 18:46). As we can also see with the apostle and **prophet** Paul, who constantly came "to visions and revelations of the Lord" (2 Corinthians 12:1; Acts 13:1). Paul was more of a marathon runner in a lifelong race—a race in which he was temperate in all things and disciplined (1 Corinthians 9:24–27). He had to use wisdom as to who and how he made his delivery as he ran. He didn't want to make his vision in vain or void; as he tells us,

> And I went up by revelation, and communicated unto them that gospel which I preach among the Gentiles, but privately to them which were of reputation, lest by any means I should run, or had run, in vain. (Galatians 2:2)

He was also a light packer, and he ran with endurance (Hebrews 12:1). He didn't need anything getting in the way of his heavenly calling. Finally, Paul fulfilled his ministry, his vision, and his commission!

> I have fought a good fight, I have finished my course, I have kept the faith. (2 Timothy 4:7)

Paul ran the course of his race, reading, writing, and speaking the vision.

> Write the vision, and make it plain upon tables, that he may run that readeth it. (Habakkuk 2:2)

He was told to make it plain on tablets and to write it in such a way that it is "understandable." The vision was intended for the runner (messenger) to read it as he ran. Our vision should be one that, once transcribed, can then be easily transferable on a transcontinental scale (if need be). Remember, if it is not understandable, the message can be lost, misinterpreted, or even twisted. "Make your vision plain, not in hieroglyphs." Simplify it so that others can easily follow it.

A child of God who is in it to win it and has taken up running with the gospel wherever it may lead and as a lifelong profession is usually one who possesses a "runner's heart." A runner's heart is a medical term that signifies that a person's heart through constant conditioning of exercise has developed a slight and healthy deviation in function. The purpose of this is so that "the heart can pump more blood around the body." It helps the individual's performance.

In similitude, the scripture says, "Exercise thyself rather unto godliness" (1 Timothy 4:7). The Christians of today receive, as they develop, a runner's heart, also known in the Holy Bible as "largeness of heart." King Solomon, the wisest man who ever lived, possessed such a heart.

> And God gave Solomon wisdom and understanding exceeding much, and **largeness of heart**, even as the sand that is on the sea shore. And Solomon's wisdom excelled the wisdom of all the children of the east country, and all the wisdom of Egypt. For he was wiser than all men; than Ethan the Ezrahite, and Heman, and Chalcol, and Darda, the sons of Mahol: and his fame was in all nations round about. (1 Kings 4:29–31, emphasis added)

The psalmist also makes mention of this runner's gift.

> I will run the way of thy commandments, when thou shalt enlarge my heart. (Psalm 119:32)

The man of God speaks about running the course of God's commandments. Of being obedient to His distinct and authoritative orders, as a derivative and by-product of his heart being enlarged.

It is the wisdom that God pours into our hearts that makes it large.

> So king Solomon exceeded all the kings of the earth for riches and for wisdom. And all the earth sought to

42

Solomon, to hear his wisdom, which God had put in his
heart. (1 Kings 10:23–24)

Why is it important to have largeness of heart? It's fundamental,
for everything comes from the heart. In Proverbs 4:23, we are instructed
to "keep thy heart with all diligence; for out of it are the issues of life."
Out of the heart spring forth the issues of life. We also already know that
the heart is the soil where the Seed of God is planted. So, in turn, we
see here that the wisdom of God has more soil to work with—a bigger
"crop, field, and plantation!" The runner, thus, produces more. How can
he not? Since he is relentlessly running to and fro, sowing the vision,
he's probably a compulsive sower that even sows on accident!

That's just what he does all day. He doesn't even tire, for "they
shall run, and not be weary" (Isaiah 40:31). A "sower"—this is just who
he is.

Out of all the knowledge, wisdom, and understanding that He pours
and funnels into our hearts, all that we need is only one Word, idea, or
plan to run with all the way up the narrow gate of success!

Through a vision of God, you'll be able to do godlike things on
earth "according to the power that worketh in us" (Ephesians 3:20) and
also through "the exceeding greatness of his power to us-ward who believe, according to the working of his mighty power, which he wrought
in Christ, when he raised him from the dead, and set him at his own right
hand in the heavenly places" (Ephesians 1:19–20). There is resurrection
power (the same power that raised Jesus from the grave) inside the gas
tank of your heart. You are being "filled with all the fulness of God"
(Ephesians 3:19), which is enough to propel the legs of your vision and
the engine of your heart so that when our Lord Jesus Christ gives you
the crown of life, you will be able to look down from heaven and see the
deep trail and canyons that your vision left behind for many to follow!

The vision is not just a vision. The vision is real and more than
reality because it is spiritual. And this message is an end-time prophecy
for the runners of today and for the upcoming ones. The timing is perfect

because some of the greatest moves of the Spirit of God were sealed for the last days, which I wholeheartedly and with all conviction believe have now been opened and released. This little book is proof of the "increase of knowledge." Trust me. I'm not that bright, but God is! "This is all God. It's all Him."

It is time for the runners to be loosed and unleashed!

> But thou, O Daniel, shut up the words, and seal the book, even to the time of the end: many shall run to and fro, and knowledge shall be increased. (Daniel 12:4)

Thus says the Spirit, "Child of God, will you run for the kingdom?"

There's an old, famous enlisting poster of former-president Abraham Lincoln, where he is depicted pointing his finger at the viewer, saying, "I want you for the US Army." In like fashion, right now the finger of God is pointing directly at you, you "the new man, which after God is created" (Ephesians 4:24). And He is saying through the Holy Spirit to your inner man, "Wake up! The world needs you."

The King of the heavenly places has called you by name.

> Then the runners went throughout all Israel and Judah with the letters from the king and his leaders, and spoke according to the command of the king. (2 Chronicles 30:6 NKJV)

The scripture says that knowledge shall increase. This is knowledge in every facet of life, but more so in the realm of the knowledge of God. The knowledge of God equates to having "ACCESS" to God. This knowledge allows us to see what we couldn't see or didn't know before.

In these latter times, "the people that do know their God shall be strong, and do exploits. And they that understand among the people shall instruct many" (Daniel 11:32–33). Those who are wise shall increase in knowledge and understanding and shall teach, lead, and build many, as

Paul the apostle, prophet, and runner did in his time and is still doing today!

Just because a mystery was shared by the writer (through the inspiration of God—God breathed) in the Book, it doesn't mean that it has been completely seized, capitalized, or fully banked upon. I believe that the following mystery is such one. So, Brother Paul, what did you want the church to understand and share with everyone, seen and unseen?

Paul wrote,

> Unto me, who am less than the least of all saints, is this grace given, that I should preach among the Gentiles the unsearchable riches of Christ; and **to make all men see** what is the fellowship of the mystery, which from the beginning of the world hath been hid in God, who created all things by Jesus Christ: to the intent that now unto the principalities and powers in heavenly places **might be made known by the church the manifold wisdom of God**, according to the eternal purpose which he purposed in Christ Jesus our Lord: in whom we have boldness and access with confidence by the faith of him. (Ephesians 3:8–12, emphasis added)

Through Christ Jesus, now the whole world has access to salvation and to the Heavenly Father, no doubt. Is that all, though?

Here, we catch Paul in full stride as he was running by preaching and delivering the unsearchable riches of Christ to the church at Ephesus and to all the churches. The main point being revealed was that now the Gentiles (all non-Jewish nationalities) could receive salvation. There's more, however, that he wanted to "make all see"… "To the intent that now the manifold wisdom of God might be made known by the church to the principalities and powers in the heavenly places" (Ephesians 3:10 NKJV). Also, now in our "Lord Jesus, we have boldness and access!"

Paul wanted the church to see, which is to <u>understand</u>, that they were to make the manyfold—the many-sided and multifaceted wisdom of God—known to the "principalities and powers" in the heavenly places. To make known to the principalities-rulers and powers-authorities, which are the "ruling authorities," the governing laws and principles of how things operate in heaven. That the church, through the variegated (*variegated*: consisting of a variety of things; multicolored or being diversified) wisdom of God, would know that they have access and authority!

What is the church to tell and make known to the governing laws and principles of heaven? Ephesians 1:3 says, "Blessed be the God and Father of our Lord Jesus Christ, who hath blessed us with all spiritual blessings in heavenly places in Christ." We are to make this known by declaring, "We as children of God, now know that we have full access, to every spiritual blessing, every promise, idea, copy, blueprint, and vision! in Christ Jesus in the heavenly places."

"We declare to the heavenly places (the unseen creation) that not only do we have access to you, but we know how to put you into practical use in our lives." In Christ, we have been given access to harness the heavens!

Child of God, right now, in this very moment, you are both down here in the seen and up there in the unseen. There, you are seated "in" Christ, Who is seated on a throne. From that position, you make it known! And know that you are speaking from a standpoint of supreme authority.

> And it shall come to pass in that day, I will hear, saith
> the LORD, I will hear the heavens, and they shall hear
> the earth. (Hosea 2:21)

"The manifold wisdom of God"—let's hold that thought and truth as we go back to the watchman for a second. Habakkuk, the watchman, wanted to see what God would tell him. He was then instructed to "write the vision and to make it plain on tablets." That's how one catches a vision. First, one hears or sees it and then catches it. You catch it by capturing it in written form. You then plan it and plant it. Thus, the heavens are now anchored on earth in seed form.

The book of Ephesians informs us that "the manifold wisdom of God is to be made known by the church." His wisdom is manysided. It's like a jewel with many facets. And so when a vision is caught or captured, we should not limit ourselves to just writing in the technical sense that we may automatically assume. Writing is vast! It's the medium through which man sets something down and then communicates it. Writing as well is manifold. There are many different types and styles. If you really think about it, the possibilities are endless.

Though the vision is to be written (captured), it can be written in various ways. The point is for us to capture the emails that God has released to man. Let's look at the different forms of writing that God ascribed to when dealing with prophetic visions and the various instructions given.

God gives blueprints, plans, and patterns to write and follow to initiate, construct, and create. Some of these consist of representations of heavenly things. For instance, of the Old Testament tabernacle and its ministry, we are told through the book of Hebrews something most interesting pertaining to its structure.

> Who serve unto the example [copy] and shadow of heavenly things, as Moses was admonished of God when he was about to make the tabernacle: for, See, saith he, that thou make all things according to the pattern shewed to thee in the mount. (Hebrews 8:5)

Moses was shown and given a pattern of the tabernacle that was stationed in heaven. It's the same one that is depicted in the book of Revelation 15:5: "And after that I looked, and, behold, the temple of the tabernacle of the testimony in heaven was opened."

47

"Moses, if you follow the pattern, your people will have a tabernacle 'on earth, as it is in heaven!'" (Glory!)

The tabernacle and its ministry were prophetic, for they pointed to Christ. It was symbolic, as scripture informs us,

> The Holy Ghost this signifying, that the way into the holiest of all was not yet made manifest, while as the first tabernacle was yet standing. (Hebrews 9:8)

Earth only holds the examples, shadows, and representations of heaven.

> But Christ came as High Priest of the good things to come, with the greater and more perfect tabernacle not made with hands, that is, not of this creation. (Hebrews 9:11 NKJV)

Yet He allowed us to momentarily have and partake in something similar, all because Moses made all things according to the pattern shown to him on the mountain.

Let us rejoice alongside the great psalmist of Israel, King David, who was blown away by the fact that God is mindful of us. He sang,

> What is man, that thou art mindful of him? and the son of man, that thou visitest him? for thou hast made him a little lower than the **angels,** and hast crowned him with glory and honour. Thou madest him to have dominion over the works of thy hands; thou hast put all things under his feet. (Psalm 8:4–6, emphasis added)

King David knew who he was in God. The word *angels* here translates to "*elohim*" in Hebrew. It is the plural name for God (the Father, the Son, and the Holy Spirit). David had the understanding that God had made him a little lower than *"elohim"* (than Himself, a little lower than God!) and made him in "His image" according to the likeness of the Trinity (Genesis 1:26). He also knew that "dominion" had not been lost in the garden of Eden because he himself ruled and reigned as king through the dominion that God had given him over all the works of His hands. King David knew that the following scripture was more real than the air he breathed:

> And God blessed them, and God said unto them, Be fruitful, and multiply, and replenish the earth, and sub-due it: and have **dominion** over the fish of the sea, and over the fowl of the air, and over every living thing that moveth upon the earth. (Genesis 1:28, emphasis added)

David also knew about blueprints, plans, and patterns (copies and shadows). When he decided that he would build a temple for the LORD, he assembled at Jerusalem all the leaders of Israel who served him from all the divisions (1 Chronicles 28:1) to communicate and convey to them his vision.

> Then David the king stood up upon his feet, and said, Hear me, my brethren, and my people: As for me, **I had in mine heart** to build an house of rest for the ark of the covenant of the LORD, and for the footstool of our God, **and had made ready for the building**: but God said unto me, Thou shalt not build an house for my name, because thou hast been a man of war, and hast shed blood. (1 Chronicles 28:2–3, emphasis added)

"David, my son, the temple shall be built, but it will be done by the hands of your son Solomon, instead." You know what the Holy Bible says about our plans? "A man's heart deviseth his way: but the LORD

49

directeth his steps" (Proverbs 16:9). The vision stayed the same; it was the strategy that changed.

We can glean three principles from this section.

- King David had a vision in his heart.
- He made preparations for the vision.
- He started telling others about the vision.

When one really wants to see their vision come to pass, there are going to be preparations made. There's going to be a deep, burning desire and passion in your heart. Then, there's also going to be movement in those feet, for the believer "catches a vision and runs with it!" spreading the word far and wide. This is our spirit and mentality. We are go-getters, and we hit the ground running! We also know how to pass the ball, as King David did to his son Solomon.

> Then David gave to Solomon his son the **pattern** of the porch, and of the houses thereof, and of the treasuries thereof, and of the upper chambers thereof, and of the inner parlours thereof, and of the place of the mercy seat, and **the pattern of all that he had by the spirit**, of the courts of the house of the LORD, and of all the chambers round about, of the treasuries of the house of God, and of the treasuries of the dedicated things. (1 Chronicles 28:11–12, emphasis added)

We're given some details of the instructions, plans, and pattern:

> Also for the courses of the priests and the Levites, and for all the work of the service of the house of the LORD, and for all the vessels of service in the house of the LORD. He gave of gold by weight for things of gold, for all instruments of all manner of service; silver also

> for all instruments of silver by weight, for all instru-
> ments of every kind of service. (1 Chronicles 28:13–14)

Included were the plans for the priests on how to perform their service to God and the designs and weights of all the articles of the lamps,
tables, forks, bowls, and cups for the basins, the altar of incense, and the
cherubim that spread out their wings and covered the ark of the covenant
of the LORD (1 Chronicles 28:15–18).

How did King David come up with all these plans and details? We
note that in verse 12, it says, "And the pattern of all that he had by the
spirit." And in verse 19, we get deeper insight:

> All this, said David, the LORD made me understand in
> writing by his hand upon me, even all the works of this
> pattern. (1 Chronicles 28:19)

Let's simplify that verse even more. David had a desire in his heart.
He grabbed a pen and parchment, and as he began writing, the Holy
Spirit took over. Then all the copies (designs) of the actual heavenly
things began to flow out like a running faucet (when we are dealing with
God the spiritual and the prophetic, you never know what will come out
through you). Next thing he knew, he was holding in his hands the plans
for one of the world's greatest wonders!

A lot, and mostly everyone, has desires, but not everyone makes the
plans, patterns, and the preparations. This is why it is essential to write it
down. It gets the process started, and sometimes your vision can at first
be like a fuzzy and foggy idea or a concept, but as you begin writing
"something" happens, the finger of God takes over. One will look at the
results and surely say, "Did I do this? This is far too extravagant!" And
by all means, please tell somebody and as many bodies as possible. King
David said, "All leaders, huddle up, I have this plan…It's game time!"

For instance, when I began writing this book, I went crazy telling
everyone on the yard, "God is going to use *The Little Seed* to cause a

worldwide revival!" How God was talking to me audibly, in my heart. And as I would be talking, we would see a plane or a private jet fly over the prison yard, and I would point my finger at it and say, "One day, I'm going to be traveling in one of those."

When you know something with your heart, nobody can tell you otherwise, and honestly, usually nobody does. They get swept away by your fervor, vision, and enthusiasm. Or maybe, and more possibly, what is really happening is that the spirit of prophecy is at work, and the Holy Spirit is bearing witness to their spirit on His behalf and yours as well.

I was so fired up that people around me got inspired just by hearing about the book. I really wanted them to have a vision for themselves, and they knew that. If God can do it for me, He can do it for anyone. If a man in prison—with no formal education, dressed in sackcloth, and with only three cents in his inmate trust account balance—can point to a private jet and say, "One day, God is going to take me all around the world," then what is stopping you from speaking your vision? Me, I couldn't stop talking about it, and I still can't (mind-blowing, boom!). I must continue sowing seeds.

My sisters and brothers dare to tap into the unlimited reservoirs of the heavenly pools of Siloam (John 9:1–15) and become a glistening oasis in the middle of a spiritless and cultural desert. Your output shall be distinctive and will draw others, like "moths unto a flame." It will have that prophetic quality that will speak directly to the souls of the masses, for it will be infused with the Holy Spirit. You shall render a "masterpiece" because the Master Himself, His very breath, shall be enmeshed in your craft.

Once the vision is captured and in the form of a plan, it becomes combustible, and since it's from God, it'll have enough power and favor to set afire the whole world!

King David sketched and drew out all the patterns and dimensions of the temple and of all the articles, which confirms that God can use the hands of an artist to minister and for prophecy.

We can see it done through the prophet Ezekiel. He was told to por-tray a city on tile, which was a wet tablet, and I wonder what the finished work looked like. It wasn't a piece of your typical abstract art; it was "prophetic" abstract art. There's a big difference. It possessed meaning, depth, and truth. The inspiration came from heaven. God said to him,

> Thou also, son of man, take thee a tile, and lay it before
> thee, and pourtray upon it the city, even Jerusalem: and
> lay siege against it, and build a fort against it, and cast
> a mount against it; set the camp also against it, and set
> battering rams against it round about. Moreover take
> thou unto thee an iron pan, and set it for a wall of iron
> between thee and the city: and set thy face against it,
> and it shall be besieged, and thou shalt lay siege against
> it. This shall be a sign to the house of Israel. (Ezekiel
> 4:1–3)

Ezekiel's artwork conveyed a message. It was a prophecy that what they were to observe was what was to come upon them.

There were instances when it wasn't the arts that one could see that spoke God's message, but instead, it was the ones that one could hear. The prophetic also works through music, through artistic melodies. The book of Psalms is filled with prophecy.

In the Old Testament, when God gave a command, it became a law. To the children of Israel, the laws of God were also the laws of the land. They were one and the same. If God said it, then they were, by reason of the law of the land, to obey it.

The LORD told Moses that His children were about to enter the land flowing with milk and honey, and once there, they would forget Him. In turn, troubles would befall them (Deuteronomy 31). God then gave Moses a prophetic song:

> Give ear, O ye heavens, and I will speak; and hear, O
> earth, the words of my mouth. My doctrine shall drop
> as the rain, my speech shall distil as the dew, as the
> small rain upon the tender herb, and as the showers
> upon the grass: because I will publish the name of the
> LORD: ascribe ye greatness unto our God. He is the
> Rock, his work is perfect: for all his ways are judgment:
> a God of truth and without iniquity, just and right is he.
> (Deuteronomy 32:1–4)

I ended the song right here, but you can read all of it in Deuteron-omy 32:1–43. The song started off sweet, but we know that the children of Israel tended to stray (and we are no different), and God changes the tone real quick and drops the hammer on them. The point of the song was that it was telling them what was going to happen in their time to come; it was pointing to what was not there yet. The song would testify against them as a witness on that day (Deuteronomy 31:21).

How many artists have sung a song, and the very same thing that they sing about is the thing that comes upon them? How much more will it come to pass when a song is given by the Spirit of God?

> Now therefore write ye this song for you, and teach it
> the children of Israel: put it in their mouths, that this
> song may be a witness for me against the children of
> Israel. (Deuteronomy 31:19)

Look at how long it took Moses to take action.

> Moses therefore wrote this song the same day, and
> taught it the children of Israel. (Deuteronomy 31:22)

Moses then wrote the song in a book where the laws were recorded (where they were captured and stored), and from there, they could and would continue to give direction and life to the readers and the hearers (Deuteronomy 31:24–26). This is a song that has been read by millions, and perhaps even billions, of people all around the world.

Then, there were times when the man of God became the sign himself. God told the prophet Ezekiel, "For I have set thee for a sign unto the house of Israel," and, "Say, I am your sign: like as I have done, so shall it be done unto them" (Ezekiel 12:6 and 11). Being the sign in those times wasn't always a pretty picture, as we shall see with the prophet Isaiah.

> And the LORD said, Like as my servant Isaiah hath walked naked and barefoot three years for a sign and wonder upon Egypt and upon Ethiopia. (Isaiah 20:3)

I'm sure that the good LORD won't ask you to do the same thing or something similar, but I can't promise it either. The point is that Isaiah was obedient, and God was able to prophesy through his life. The prophets' responsibility was to declare what God had shown him, as he, "the prophet," tells us:

> For thus hath the Lord said unto me, Go, set a watchman, let him declare what he seeth. (Isaiah 21:6)

But I'm not talented, gifted, or skilled enough to do something great, you might be thinking or saying to yourself. God's response to you is, "You have no clue what I have placed inside of you! But I'm going to show you." I can tell you that "if you have received Christ, you have the Holy Spirit taking residence inside of your heart" (Galatians 4:6). This fact is our bedrock.

After Moses was given the pattern for the tabernacle, God didn't dust His hands and say, "You are on your own now." On the contrary, He made sure that those plans would be carried out.

Everything that has to do with God is much bigger than us, and He has to help us. He does it by stirring us through His Spirit for the work at hand. Let's get into the fine print of that event.

> And the LORD spake unto Moses, saying, See, I have called by name Bezaleel the son of Uri, the son of Hur, of the tribe of Judah: and I have filled him with the spirit of God, in wisdom, and in understanding, and in knowledge, and in all manner of workmanship, to devise cunning works, to work in gold, and in silver, and in brass, and in cutting of stones, to set them, and in carving of timber, to work in all manner of workmanship. And I, behold, I have given with him Aholiab, the son of Ahisamach, of the tribe of Dan: and in the hearts of all that are wise hearted I have put wisdom, that they may make all that I have commanded thee. (Exodus 31:1–6)

Within the span of these six verses, we notice that God used the word *I* six times. He says, "*I* have filled him with the spirit of God," and "In the hearts of all that are wise hearted *I* have put wisdom, that they may make all that *I* have commanded thee." And as a result of His Spirit and His wisdom, being put into His children, they in turn were able to do all kinds of workmanship and all manner of artistic works! God had to enable them.

You, on the other hand, are already able. You can do all things through Christ, Who strengthens you! (Philippians 4:13). It is Christ Who gives you strength! As we have already established, you have the Holy Spirit living inside of you. As a matter of fact, you have been sealed with the Spirit of God, which means that it's a done deal. He is with you and in you, and He has your back for life (the Comforter!). You have His help (2 Corinthians 1:22; John 14:16–17).

> And because ye are sons, God hath sent forth the Spirit
> of his Son into your hearts, crying, Abba, Father. (Ga-
> latians 4:6)

The Spirit from within our hearts cries out, "Daddy! Father!" But
have you considered that the Spirit also cries out and pleads with "us,"
wanting to use "us"? "For it is God which worketh in you both to will
and to do of his good pleasure" (Philippians 2:13). Grieving the Holy
Spirit can be done in many ways. "And grieve not the holy Spirit of God,
whereby ye are sealed unto the day of redemption" (Ephesians 4:30).
Allow the Spirit to work through your life. Let Him do His thing! "Not
my will, but thine, be done" (Luke 22:42).

The Holy Spirit will give you all the knowledge, wisdom, and understanding that you need. The very same Spirit that was inside Jesus is
in you right now.

> And the spirit of the LORD shall rest upon him, the
> spirit of wisdom and understanding, the spirit of coun-
> sel and might, the spirit of knowledge and of the fear of
> the LORD. (Isaiah 11:2)

And if having God's Spirit weren't enough, remember how Moses
wrote that prophetic song in the book and it became law? (To which,
concerning God's law, Jesus said it cannot be broken, meaning that "if
that's what the scripture says, then that's what it is" (John 10:35). There
is no changing with God's Word.) Well, our Heavenly "Abba-Father"
has done something greater with you! He has written His Word on the
tablet of your heart (a prophetic Word, at that), so what could possibly
hold you back? He has given it all to you on a silver platter.

> For this is the covenant that I will make with the house
> of Israel [and the church] after those days, saith the
> Lord; I will put my laws into their mind, and write them

57

in their hearts: and I will be to them a God, and they
shall be to me a people. (Hebrews 8:10)

That Word is not written on tile, clay tablets, or in a book, nor is it written by man; it's written by God. And if it's God's Word, we know that it cannot be broken, and it's also "law and binding," which means that it provides you with all heavenly legal access to all that has been allotted to His children. Jesus said, "The words that I speak unto you, they are spirit, and they are life" (John 6:63). Thus, while we do our best to write the Word on our hearts, through meditation and repetition (planting it), it only agrees with what God has already written. It agrees and comes together, being confirmed by the Spirit.

You are well able! You have what is needed and what it takes. The Holy Bible teaches us to "let this mind be in you, which was also in Christ Jesus" (Philippians 2:5). You have the mind of Christ available. Let it work for you! Use it!

Now because the Holy Spirit in you is "multifaceted" (Revelation 1:4) and the wisdom of God that is in you is "manifold/variegated," this makes you, my friend, "versatile" by divine nature! The Christ in you is ready to burst out on the scene and make a magnificent spectacle through your God-given abilities and potential.

The genius of God, His brilliance and splendor, is trapped inside you, and He is unleashed and set free through a vision. Still, you will always need a blueprint, and that's why your vision needs to be captured and written in the form of a plan.

O LORD, how manifold are thy works! in wisdom
hast thou made them all: the earth is full of thy riches.
(Psalm 104:24)

And it is that same creative wisdom, with which He created all things, that He has poured into your heart and filled you with.

> And Moses called Bezaleel and Aholiab, and every
> wise hearted man, in whose heart the LORD had put
> wisdom, even every one whose heart stirred him up to
> come unto the work to do it. (Exodus 36:2)

Child of God, know and understand that not only are you His finger, His paintbrush, and His pigment, but you are also the canvas through which He portrays and displays His power, glory, and majesty here on earth.

You are His unique and one-of-a-kind masterpiece. There's no one like you on earth, and there never will be. He has embossed you with His fingerprint, from which I deduce that of His, no two are alike. If you were to do an accurate self-analysis, you'd discover that you are incomparable and without equal or rival. This fact alone makes you a rarity, and your value is priceless.

So why do you, as a gem, have to be a "one and only" and a spectacle of spectacles? The reason is that God is fulfilling His plan. He is personally building a building, which is a house and a temple. We've seen that Moses built the tabernacle and King Solomon built the temple. But you and I are involved in something more spectacular and magnificent. This time, His children are not the ones doing the building; this time, we are the ones being built—we are the building!

> Now therefore ye are no more strangers and foreigners,
> but fellowcitizens with the saints, and of the household
> of God; and are built upon the foundation of the apos-
> tles and prophets, Jesus Christ himself being the chief
> corner stone; in whom all the building fitly framed to-
> gether groweth unto an holy temple in the Lord. (Ephe-
> sians 2:19–21)

This temple is different, for it is spiritual, and because it is spiritual, it's on a whole 'nother level, a heavenly one! Do you want to see what every individual stone looks like up close?

> [The Son] To whom coming, as unto [The Father] a living stone, dissallowed indeed of men, but chosen of God, and precious, ye also, as lively stones, are built up a spiritual house, an holy priesthood, to offer up spiritual sacrifices, acceptable to God by Jesus Christ. (1 Peter 2:4–5)

You are also, as Christ did, coming to the Father as living stones and are being built up into a spiritual house—into a temple where every stone bears a resemblance to Jesus. Don't worry; it's a growing process, like when a baby is born. Ultimately, Christ will be formed in you (Galatians 4:19).

This temple is mobile, and it is made up of many distinct and individual parts (living stones), which are spread out throughout the whole earth. So that wherever we find ourselves, we are to personally lay claim in the mighty name of Jesus and "set up shop" as both "king and priest" and exercise our dominion as we proclaim Christ and His kingdom through His Word, the Spirit, and our vision. Isn't that awesome?

> But ye are a chosen generation, a royal priesthood, an holy nation, a peculiar people; that ye should shew forth the praises of him who hath called you out of darkness into his marvellous light. (1 Peter 2:9)

Through these pages and the coming ones, the Spirit of God has been giving you personal prophecy, speaking to your heart, saying that "as He did with the life of Christ, so shall the Father do with your life." He wants to reveal His Son in you in that He wants our lives to be a picture of Jesus. As the apostle Paul stated, "For I bear in my body the marks of the Lord Jesus" (Galatians 6:17).

Paul did not hold it in. He made it known by committing the mysteries of God to one and all! He said, "For I have received of the Lord that which also I delivered unto you" (1 Corinthians 11:23), and "I am made all things to all men, that I might by all means save some" (1 Corinthians 9:22).

All the options, avenues, and styles and all the projects, plans, and patterns of heaven are open and at your disposal. There's no limit to how you can allow God to make it happen through your many talents. Just put your hand on the plow and don't look back. What talents? The ones that you are loaded with!

"Now concerning spiritual gifts, brethren, I would not have you ignorant" (1 Corinthians 12:1):

> Now there are diversities of gifts, but the same Spirit. And there are differences of administrations, but the same Lord. And there are diversities of operations, but it is the same God which worketh all in all. But the manifestation of the Spirit is given to every man to profit withal. For to one is given by the Spirit the word of wisdom; to another the word of knowledge by the same Spirit; to another faith by the same Spirit; to another the gifts of healing by the same Spirit; to another the working of miracles; to another prophecy; to another discerning of spirits; to another divers kinds of tongues; to another the interpretation of tongues: but all these worketh that one and the selfsame Spirit, dividing to every man severally as he will. For as the body is one, and hath many members, and all the members of that one body, being many, are one body: so also is Christ.
> (1 Corinthians 12:4–12)

There are diversities of talents and different ministries (administrations), and there are diversities of operations and activities. The Holy Spirit supplies it all. There's so much wisdom and knowledge. He distributes gifts of healing, miracles, and prophecy! You can write the vision, draw the vision, and sing the vision. You can even be the vision! Nor is the manifold wisdom of God limited to the illustrations rendered in this chapter and book, for His wisdom and His manner of work are too vast and boundless. That's why your works shall be of unparalleled magnitude. You shall literally present and dispense the works of God to the populace. The apostle Paul professed that the gospel that he was presenting to the brethren and the churches, "which they were hearing," was not from him but that it came to him directly from God. Jesus made it known to him by way of revelation.

> But I certify you, brethren, that the gospel which was
> preached of me is not after man. For I neither received
> it of man, neither was I taught it, but by the revelation
> of Jesus Christ. (Galatians 1:11–12)

Imagine how certain individuals responded to his message. Here, he was proclaiming that the Spirit of God had revealed to him wisdom and mysteries that had been hidden since the beginning of time and how now, through this gospel, they were hearing, they, too, would have the same understanding of the said knowledge. Wow! "That's big vision talk." And today, we know that what he received and made known was in fact "by the Word of the Lord." (When God gives you a vision, it's sure to be a winner!)

> For this cause I Paul, the prisoner of Jesus Christ for
> you Gentiles, if ye have heard of the dispensation of
> the grace of God which is given me to you-ward: how
> that by revelation he made known unto me the mystery;
> (as I wrote afore in few words, whereby, when ye read,

ye may understand my knowledge in the mystery of
Christ) which in other ages was not made known unto
the sons of men, as it is now revealed unto his holy
apostles and prophets by the Spirit. (Ephesians 3:1–5)

He said, "It was given to me for you." There's a purpose for your
gift. It's so that you can reach others. Look at how many enumerable
souls Paul reached and touched that have received and entered into everlasting life as a consequence of "making known" the revelations (visions) of God. He ran, and he ran well! "Paul the apostle, we as the
church commend you."

Habakkuk wrote the vision, Paul wrote the vision, and I wrote
mine. Now it's your turn. "Your vision doesn't start when people see it.
It begins when you do." And a vision is not a vision until you write it
down. For God said to the prophet, "Write the vision."

Heaven will never run out of fresh material. I dare say that if you
search for them, "He'll renew your visions every morning!" The vision
is for others, so just give them what God has committed to you. He will
not send you out without first imparting it to you. The runner was always
given something to hold on to as he ran. Now here you hold in your
hands "the little seed." Use it as encouragement as you run and tell the
world that "Jesus is coming back."

I pray in Jesus's name that He multiplies your visions. God has said
in His Word,

I have also spoken by the prophets, and I have multiplied visions, and used similitudes, by the ministry of
the prophets. (Hosea 12:10)

Also, may the Father give you more hope and courage so that you
may valiantly express the vision that He has placed in your heart. I pray
for you the same prayer that the apostle Paul asked for himself as he
prayed with all prayer and supplication:

And for me, that utterance may be given unto me, that
I may open my mouth boldly, to make known the mystery of the gospel. (Ephesians 6:19)

Sons and daughters of the kingdom (little seeds), hear me. Hear the
Spirit speaking through me. You've always wanted more, and you've always felt that somehow you were going to make it. Well, here it is! This
is your chance. This is your shot. "Go for it!" And with all boldness,
make it known.

God is faithful. "If you write it, He will light it." Now run with the
Olympic torch (which has been lit with the heavenly fire of Mount Zion)
all over the world and as far as your vision will take you! Run in such
a way that ye may obtain the prize (1 Corinthians 9:24), which is the
crown of glory (1 Peter 5:4), a crown that fadeth not away!

THE VISION OF HABAKKUK

Then the LORD answered me and said: "Write the vision and make it plain on tablets, that he may run who reads it."

—Habakkuk 2:2 NKJV

_____

_____

_____

_____

_____

_____

_____

_____

_____

_____

_____

_____

_____

_____

_____

_____

_____

_____

_____

_____

_____

_____

_____

CHAPTER 5

THE VISION OF METHUSELAH

Methuselah was the oldest recorded person to have ever lived on earth. According to the book of Genesis, he lived 969 years, and he died (Genesis 5:27). So what does he have to do with "vision, seeds, and manifestation; of things coming to pass?" Well, I had always heard from word of mouth that a clay pot that contained seeds had been found in a pharaoh's tomb, and upon picking it up, a seed fell out of it and hit the ground; it fell upon the soil. With time, it then began to sprout, blossom, and bloom. This story always amazed me because I always related it to the power of the Word. So many scriptures come to mind: "Being born again, not of corruptible seed, but of incorruptible, by the word of God, which liveth and abideth for ever" (1 Peter 1:23), "For the word of God is living and powerful" (Hebrews 4:12 NKJV), and "Heaven and earth shall pass away, but my words shall not pass away" (Matthew 24:35).

A few nights ago, while watching a Christian show on television, I thought that I had finally heard the true and accurate story. In 1963, while excavation was taking place on the ruins of the fortress mountaintop of Masada, which is located on the shore of the Dead Sea, a clay pot was discovered, and it contained seeds inside. They were of a Judean palm tree, whose class at one point had become extinct. The seeds date back approximately two thousand years.

Around the same time, in AD 73, a sorrowful catastrophe occurred on top of Masada. God's chosen people made their last stand there in

67

revolt and opposition to the Roman legions, where they all ended their lives. Life on top of Masada was lost, so it seemed.

The seeds were discovered in 1963; however, it wasn't until 2005 that one was planted, and lo and behold, it sprouted! The date palm tree was named Methuselah, and today, his pollen is being used to make others after his own kind. What had been thought to be over forever and not seen can now not only be seen but also held and tasted! It can now even be reproduced on a mass scale.

> Is the seed still in the barn? As yet the vine, the fig tree, the pomegranate, and the olive tree have not yielded fruit. But from this day I will bless you. (Haggai 2:19 NKJV)

One could've said of the Methuselah seed, "What is the seed still doing in a vault, a laboratory, or a museum? You mean that it was hidden, lost, or kept secret for two millennia, and you are still going to hold it back some more? Somebody plant it already!"

In the same way, God can say to us, "What is My seed (Word) still doing in the barn (in the Book)?" The seed shouldn't be in the barn, but it should be planted in our hearts, and then we are to go out into the field of the world and continue sowing seeds. The more we plant, the more He will give us. "Now may He who supplies seed to the sower, and bread for food, supply and multiply the seed you have sown and increase the fruits of your righteousness" (2 Corinthians 9:10 NKJV).

Even before you plant the seed, the seed itself is already blessed. God says that your vine, your fig tree, your pomegranate, and your olive tree are already in full fruition, ready for you in the future. "From this day will I bless you" (Haggai 2:19). And if you can see it, then God has just given you a vision! All that you have to do is "get your seed out of the barn."

Earlier in the first chapter, we spoke about billions upon billions of spiritual shelves holding our blessings in heavenly places. We can liken that to a "seed still in the barn."

Visions—still in the barn. Dreams—still in the barn. A much better and greater version of us—still in the barn. Promises, blessings, miracles, and prophecies—still in the barn. Ideas, plans and patterns, artistic masterpieces, and musical works—still in the barn. "All things that pertain unto life and godliness" (2 Peter 1:3) are all seeds still in the barn. What about "your" seed? Is your seed still in the barn? Are we seeds still inside a clay pot, or are we seeds already planted in the soil?

The Methuselah seed had been patiently waiting for two thousand years, but just eight weeks after it had been planted, it began to grow, and the first shoots were showing. This type of date palm tree also has the potential to reach heights of eighty feet in the air! For many of you, it'll be the same happenstance.

And obviously, it was named Methuselah because of its old age. You and I don't have the same luxury of sitting around waiting forever. Our time is running out. The clock is ticking! We've been delayed for far too long. The waiting time is over!

It is time to rise high!

It is time to get our vision out there!

THE VISION OF METHUSELAH

Then the LORD answered me and said: "Write the vision and make it plain on tablets, that he may run who reads it."

—Habakkuk 2:2 NKJV

_____
_____
_____
_____
_____
_____
_____
_____
_____
_____
_____
_____
_____
_____
_____
_____
_____
_____
_____
_____
_____
_____
_____

CHAPTER 6

CREATED FOR VISION

Heavenly Father, in the name of Jesus Christ and through the power of the Holy Spirit, we ask You to bless the reading, hearing, and sharing of this word. Wonderful Father, to You be all the honor, glory, and praise. And we thank You in advance for the hundredfold increase. In Jesus's name, we pray, amen!

"For we walk by faith, not by sight" (2 Corinthians 5:7). That's true. In fact, it's scripture. However, to walk with purpose, we must have a sense of direction, and this is what a vision does. It gives us spiritual sight, but not necessarily the kind that might be readily grasped tangibly. Nevertheless, in faith, we march toward its mark, "knowing" in our hearts that He (God), Who promised, is faithful.

Let us remember that Abraham was super old when our Heavenly Father painted for him that beyond-your-wildest-dreams picture on that appointed night when he received a vision!

> And he brought him forth abroad, and said, Look now toward heaven, and tell the stars, if thou be able to number them: and he said unto him, So shall thy seed be. (Genesis 15:5)

I can imagine that every night, when he looked at the stars by faith, he could see much more and beyond what everybody else could see. He could see the promises of God. (When he looked at the stars, he could see his seeds—his descendants!) Millions of people throughout history have looked upon the same stars—some looked at them for admiration while others have used them for direction, like using a compass for navigation. This man used the stars as a daily reminder, one that drew him and pulled him into fulfilling his God-given vision—his destiny.

Abraham, in faith, looked toward his vision, not his condition. He focused on God's Word, not on his body's weakness! The scripture says,

> Who against hope believed in hope, that he might become the father of many nations, according to that which was spoken, So shall thy seed be. And being not weak in faith, he considered not his own body now dead, when he was about an hundred years old, neither yet the deadness of Sarah's womb: he staggered not at the promise of God through unbelief; but was strong in faith, giving glory to God; and being fully persuaded that, what he had promised, he was able also to perform. (Romans 4:18–21)

If God said it, that settles it!

The vision will guide our steps. For it is said of Moses that he found greater riches in Christ (he sought a Christ Who wouldn't make His full physical presentation on earth for over a thousand years). Moses looked at the reward (Hebrews 11:26).

> By faith he forsook Egypt, not fearing the wrath of the king: for he endured, as seeing him who is invisible. (Hebrews 11:27)

Question? How did Moses look? Did he do it with his natural eyes? No, it was through faith in what the LORD had revealed to him that he was able to look forward, far above and beyond his current circumstances—even those of his personal feelings, emotions, and heartaches. His vision was bigger than his now.

Our LORD, our God, this vision is far too immense for us to deliver on our own. We are going to need Your help to birth it. Because one thing is for certain: We are pregnant with Your Seed, and You are a God Who will never leave us nor forsake us. Therefore, come what may, we are pressing forward!

In the words of Christ's mother,

> Behold the handmaid of the Lord; be it unto me according to thy word. (Luke 1:38)

Lord, "have Your way, and use this broken earthen vessel, my God, for Your glory! I surrender to You my heart and my life."

"My chosen child, I can hear you."

> Behold, thou shalt call a nation that thou knowest not, and nations that knew not thee shall run unto thee because of the LORD thy God, and for the Holy One of Israel; for he hath glorified thee. (Isaiah 55:5)

My child, "there is a nation and a vision with your name on it."

> For we are his workmanship, created in Christ Jesus unto good works, which God hath before ordained that we should walk in them. (Ephesians 2:10)

The good works are already there (since before the foundations of the earth were created). He has laid it all out for us, giving us the red-carpet treatment. It is now up to us to walk in the vision.

CREATED FOR VISION

Then the LORD answered me and said: "Write the vision and make it plain on tablets, that he may run who reads it."

—Habakkuk 2:2 NKJV

_____
_____
_____
_____
_____
_____
_____
_____
_____
_____
_____
_____
_____
_____
_____
_____
_____
_____
_____
_____
_____
_____
_____
_____
_____
_____

HAVE YOU WRITTEN THE VISION

Mr. "Jesse's Place," why is all of this about vision? The Holy Bible already told us that "My [His] people are destroyed for lack of knowledge" (Hosea 4:6), for lack of vision. And "where there is no vision, the people perish" (Proverbs 29:18). When there is no vision, the people don't care; they cast off restraint, and anything goes, right?

Yes, you are right. But honestly, do we all have a vision for this year and for the years to come? I'm sure that most do. Even if it's vague, I don't doubt it. The key question is, "Have you written it down, though?"

You see, despite what you may reason, you are not alone, and I am not alone. We are one—same God, same Holy Bible, same breath, same heartbeat! (Can we be united through love?) "We" are trying to get things done, like helping people, kicking self-destructive habits, starting businesses, or getting laws passed. "We" are trying to evangelize and change the world!

For the walls of Jericho to have fallen, the marching had to be done with "one accord" (down here), and after the blast/sound of the last trumpet, God (from up there) took care of the rest and tore those walls down! (Joshua 6:15–20). "Can two walk together, except they be agreed?" (Amos 3:3). We know that a house divided will not stand.

There is invincible power in the unity of mind, purpose, and, yes, vision. The Holy Bible says,

Though one may be overpowered by another, two can withstand him. And a threefold cord is not quickly broken. (Ecclesiastes 4:12 NKJV)

For where two or three are gathered together in my name, there am I in the midst of them. (Matthew 18:20)

Remember the ten virgins? In that parable, five virgins were wise, and the other five were considered foolish. The foolish ones ended up missing out because they made light of things; they didn't take their calling seriously, and as a result, the door of blessing was closed on them.

Then shall the kingdom of heaven be likened unto ten virgins, which took their lamps, and went forth to meet the bridegroom. And five of them were wise, and five were foolish. They that were foolish took their lamps, and took no oil with them: but the wise took oil in their vessels with their lamps. While the bridegroom tarried, they all slumbered and slept. And at midnight there was a cry made, Behold, the bridegroom cometh; go ye out to meet him. Then all those virgins arose, and trimmed their lamps. And the foolish said unto the wise, Give us of your oil; for our lamps are gone out. But the wise answered, saying, Not so; lest there be not enough for us and you: but go ye rather to them that sell, and buy for yourselves. And while they went to buy, the bridegroom came; and they that were ready went in with him to the marriage: and the door was shut. Afterward came also the other virgins, saying, Lord, Lord, open to us. But he answered and said, Verily I say unto you, I know you not. Watch therefore, for ye know neither the day nor the hour wherein the Son of man cometh. (Matthew 25:1–13)

The team of the five virgins that stuck together, which were on point and were found ready, entered the kingdom and were in the presence of the King.

We know that the five wise virgins had oil in their lamps, while the five foolish virgins didn't. No oil means no light, and at night, they literally could not see; therefore, they had no "vision." If the story (parable) would've been about "writing the vision," it would've gone something like, "The five wise virgins wrote the vision, and the five foolish ones didn't."

The main point is that there is no time to put anything off because "we don't know when it's gonna go down." You know what they say? It's "the little foxes, that spoil the vines" (Song of Solomon 2:15). Like the little fox of procrastination, "it's the little things that make the big difference!"

The vision is for everyone, but will everyone be wise enough to write (catch) it?

HAVE YOU WRITTEN THE VISION

Then the LORD answered me and said: "Write the vision and make it plain on tablets, that he may run who reads it."

—Habakkuk 2:2 NKJV

_____

CHAPTER 8

FIGHT FOR YOUR VISION

When the prophet Nehemiah was "released" from captivity to repair the walls and gates of Jerusalem, every man and woman did their part. They were all building, with one goal in mind, and following the same blueprint. They all had the same vision, and God prospered them. And they were successful.

It is time! We have no choice. The adversary has been overpowering us for far too long. We must band together as the scripture says, and we must get equipped to be victorious.

The haters tried to stop Nehemiah and his people. The opposition rose, fueled by the devil, death threats, and all. And what was his response?

> And I looked, and rose up, and said unto the nobles, and to the rulers, and to the rest of the people, Be not ye afraid of them: remember the LORD, which is great and terrible, and fight for your brethren, your sons, and your daughters, your wives, and your houses. (Nehemiah 4:14)

My people, we are in a real fight. We are going somewhere, and we know where we are going; and help us, God, we are going to get there.

JESSE SUAREZ

The vision is not for me alone, nor is it for you alone. It's for one another; it's for our sons and daughters (my Zoe-mama), for our wives, and for our husbands. It's for our freedom; it's for our future and for the future of those who shall come after us. We are all moving ahead as one wave; therefore, it is very important that every single one of us has a vision and that we be ready to make a stand for it.

Be ready to make a defense.

FIGHT FOR YOUR VISION

Then the LORD answered me and said: "Write the vision and make it plain on tablets, that he may run who reads it."

—Habakkuk 2:2 NKJV

_____

_____

_____

_____

_____

_____

_____

_____

_____

_____

_____

_____

_____

_____

_____

_____

_____

_____

_____

_____

_____

_____

_____

_____

_____

CHAPTER 9

BIG VISION

I tell the men here in the prison yard that this place can't hold them because their vision is too big. And when your vision is too big, it'll work like a giant electromagnet! Just like the best commercial vacuum cleaner, it'll yank them out and pull them right out of here. It'll spit them out, place them in a business suit, and in the day of tomorrow, have them advocating for prison reform in the White House. It'll launch them to the other side of the globe and have them preaching the gospel of Jesus Christ. It'll fling them into the arms of an amazing wife with whom they can begin a family. A big vision can do that and more. A big vision can change your life as well, whoever and wherever you are. "It will not lie."

It pulled Nelson Mandela (God rest his soul) out of a prison cell and sat him on a seat of the presidency! The same thing transpired in the life of the Patriarch Joseph. The vision was so big that his parents' home couldn't hold him; he was pulled out of there! For sure, it was bigger than the pit he was thrown into, for it pulled him out of there too. Potiphar's wife's arms couldn't hold him, and through the power of God, he was able to break loose! Potiphar's house couldn't hold him, and for sure, the prison he was thrown into couldn't hold him. Back to back, from glory to glory, it pulled him out.

> Then Pharaoh sent and called Joseph, and they brought
> him hastily out of the dungeon: and he shaved himself,
> and changed his raiment, and came in unto Pharaoh.
> (Genesis 41:14)

Imagine that, within hours, Joseph had a fresh shave, a new set of clothes, and was about to receive a whole new identity. He went from the prison to the palace!

> And Pharaoh said unto Joseph, See, I have set thee
> over all the land of Egypt. And Pharaoh took off his
> ring from his hand, and put it upon Joseph's hand, and
> arrayed him in vestures of fine linen, and put a gold
> chain about his neck; and he made him ride in the sec-
> ond chariot which he had; and they cried before him,
> Bow the knee: and he made him ruler over all the land
> of Egypt. And Pharaoh said unto Joseph, I am Pharaoh,
> and without thee shall no man lift up his hand or foot in
> all the land of Egypt. (Genesis 41:41–44)

He became the governor of Egypt. He went from tending the sheep to leading the world's strongest superpower of that day and time. That would be similar to going from being a young gang member to becoming the vice president of the United States of America. From the housing projects to the presidential White House!

I know that it may sound unrealistic, but Abraham Lincoln did it. Though he was born into poverty in a log cabin, it didn't stop him from becoming president. He went on to become one of the greatest leaders that this nation has ever had. They say that it's not so amazing that he was born in a log cabin, but what was truly amazing and remarkable was that he was able to make it out of the log cabin—out of that box, the box of a mindset. And yes, the vision pulled him out!

Remember that the vision has to go beyond our current parameters. If anybody has ever had an immense vision, it was Jesus Christ. I can vividly visualize Him saying to Himself every day and every night, 24-7, "The cross, the cross, I must save the world, the cross, the cross!" and "I must die, in order, so that those who shall believe in me can live."

> For God sent not his Son into the world to condemn the world; but that the world through him might be saved. (John 3:17)

Did you know that our Jesus was in prison too? (Isaiah 53:8; Matthew 27:15–17). He was there only for a few hours, but He was too big! So God pulled Him out. The grave, the end of the line, the place of no more hope, could only retain Him for three days, but He was too big! Our God pulled Him out and up! He pulled Him up alive. He pulled Him up and resurrected Him!

> Ye men of Israel, hear these words; Jesus of Nazareth, a man approved of God among you by miracles and wonders and signs, which God did by him in the midst of you, as ye yourselves also know: whom God hath raised up, having loosed the pains of death: because it was not possible that he should be holden of it. (Acts 2:22 and 24)

Jesus was just too big—so big that nothing on earth could hold Him, and He was then pulled up to heaven.

How big is your vision?

BIG VISION

Then the LORD answered me and said: "Write the vision and make it plain on tablets, that he may run who reads it."

—Habakkuk 2:2 NKJV

_____

_____
_____
_____
_____
_____
_____
_____
_____
_____
_____
_____
_____
_____
_____
_____
_____
_____
_____
_____
_____

CHAPTER 10

CHRISTLIKENESS IS THE VISION

So did Jesus have a vision, or was He the Vision? The answer to that question is "yes"; it's both. He did have a vision, and He was and is the Vision. To be like Jesus Christ is the ultimate vision for believers. Our vision is to be entwined with Jesus, and it should lead us to a closer fellowship with Him. Every Christian should gradually move toward a life of Christlikeness. The Holy Bible says that "as he is, so are we in this world" (1 John 4:17). Therefore, when we apply the scriptures to our daily situations and activities, Christ is reflected.

We are called to do and say what He would, in any and all settings, causing His love to be seen in our visage. The apostle Paul said,

> Be ye followers of me, even as I also am of Christ. (1 Corinthians 11:1)

For now, we are to follow and imitate Christ. But one day, we, too, will be pulled up to heaven by the same Spirit, power, and God Who raised Christ from the grave, and then we shall be completely transformed into His image. That's "we [us] which are alive and remain unto the coming of the Lord" (1 Thessalonians 4:15–17) and those which shall arise from their graves.

> For now we see through a glass, darkly [dimly], but
> then face to face: now I know in part; but then shall I
> know even as also I am known. (1 Corinthians 13:12)

All of this was decided by our Heavenly Father from the realm of eternity.

> For whom he did foreknow, he also did predestinate to
> be conformed to the image of his Son, that he might be
> the firstborn among many brethren. (Romans 8:29)

Wow! Just to think that one day we shall be like our God and Big Brother Jesus tells us one thing: There is a tremendous promise, possibility, and explosive potential for growth inside us and for our future. While here on earth, we will always strive to be like Him. However, the day will come when we will cease this effort. Because as He is and where He is, that's what we will be like (in its fullness) and where we will be for eternity—forever like Him and with Him!

Apple seeds become apple trees. Orange seeds become orange trees. You and I—we are predestined to become like Jesus Christ. Our Father would not have told us this if it weren't true. Jesus is the original, and we are His carbon copies.

Brother Jesse, "Come on now, even you have to admit and agree that this 'vision' to be conformed into the image of Christ, while here on earth, is far too great."

Exactly! "And that's how we want it because it lets us know that for this one, we won't be able to do it in our own strength. We are going to need the power of God since it's a venture beyond human capability."

We are to write the vision, get it in our hearts through meditation, and make preparation. Then we leave the rest to Him. He said that "He would hasten it," and because He is the one doing it, it's going to be at the perfect time.

Being confident of this very thing, that he which hath
begun a good work in you will perform it until the day
of Jesus Christ. (Philippians 1:6)

Our Heavenly Father has given us His Word. He has already given us the seed and the vision, it's now on us to receive it and truly believe it. How will it grow? "Let's leave the hard stuff to him."

And he said, So is the kingdom of God, as if a man
should cast seed into the ground; and should sleep, and
rise night and day, and the seed should spring and grow
up, he knoweth not how. For the earth bringeth forth
fruit of herself; first the blade, then the ear, after that
the full corn in the ear. But when the fruit is brought
forth, immediately he putteth in the sickle, because the
harvest is come. (Mark 4:26–29)

And the child grew, and waxed strong in spirit, filled
with wisdom: and the grace of God was upon him.
(Luke 2:40)

Today is a new day, and you are beginning a new chapter in your life. You have a lot to look forward to.

Therefore if any man be in Christ, he is a new creature:
old things are passed away; behold, all things are become new. (2 Corinthians 5:17)

Jesus went through the process and grew into His vision, and so will you. It doesn't matter if it never worked before; this is a totally different thing.

YOU ARE A NEW CREATION! All things have become new.

CHRISTLIKENESS IS THE VISION

Then the LORD answered me and said: "Write the vision and make it plain on tablets, that he may run who reads it."

—Habakkuk 2:2 NKJV

_____

_____

_____

_____

_____

_____

_____

_____

_____

_____

_____

_____

_____

_____

_____

_____

_____

_____

_____

_____

_____

VISION BEGINS IN SEED FORM

Jesus began from being born and lying in a manger to saying in triumph on the cross, "It is finished!" and then sitting as Majesty on a heavenly throne—thus becoming the King of kings and the Lord of lords forever.

Do not get caught up in how things look right now. Visions always begin in seed form. As long as you hold your grip on it, it'll have life and grow.

> For who hath despised the day of small things? (Zechariah 4:10)

An infant never remains immature; it is not in his nature to do so. A baby becomes a child, a child becomes a juvenile, he becomes a minor, and then finally he becomes a man and reproduces children of his own.

> A little one shall become a thousand, and a small one
> a strong nation: I the LORD will hasten it in his time.
> (Isaiah 60:22)

He will hasten it. "Get it crackin'," and do it swiftly in his time (its time and "His" time) in due season. Take this seriously, though, because having a "vision" is how dreams come true and are made. The course of your life depends on it. So give it all you've got and do it now that you can. You already have everything that you need to make it happen, which is Christ in you, the hope of what...? (Yes! The hope of glory! You are learning.) (Colossians 1:27).

Every morning you wake up, thank God, say your prayers, meditate on your vision, and be fixed within your heart that no matter what happens throughout the day, you will throw your best punches!

> Whatsoever thy hand findeth to do, do it with thy might; for there is no work, nor device, nor knowledge, nor wisdom, in the grave, whither thou goest. I returned, and saw under the sun, that the race is not to the swift, nor the battle to the strong, neither yet bread to the wise, nor yet riches to men of understanding, nor yet favour to men of skill; **but time and chance happeneth to them all**. (Ecclesiastes 9:10–11, emphasis added)

Never stop, let go, or quit.

> For the vision is yet for an appointed time, but at the end it shall speak, and not lie: though it tarry, wait for it; because it will surely come, it will not tarry. (Habakkuk 2:3)

Keep those arms swinging because "your" day is coming! It is written on God's calendar.

VISION BEGINS IN SEED FORM

Then the LORD answered me and said: "Write the vision and make it plain on tablets, that he may run who reads it."

—Habakkuk 2:2 NKJV

_____

_____

_____

_____

_____

_____

_____

_____

_____

_____

_____

_____

_____

_____

_____

_____

_____

_____

_____

_____

_____

_____

CHAPTER 12

SOW THE VISION IN YOUR HEART

I know that I said, "The vision will give you vision to see." At the same time, it may be hard for you to see, envision, or premeditate something better for tomorrow. That's why you are to write it down, and as you are writing it, the desires that our God has placed in your heart will begin to flow out.

He hath set the world in their heart. (Ecclesiastes 3:11)

You would be blown away if you knew how much unlimited creativity and talent are latent and embedded in your heart, for there in the heart is where the cradle of your imagination is found. It is through your imagination that you can give conception to your dreams, your visions, and the future of your choosing.

This is a sacred place where you can see it before it happens, and in faith, you receive it as done. Knowing that, without any limitations, whatever you can see in your heart and believe, our God in heaven will give it to you, and He will do it with all gladness.

One must see it on the inside through the mind of the heart before it comes to pass and has it on the outside. Why is this of value to me and my growth, change, and transformation? Let's refresh our spirits.

1. The things that are seen were not made of things that do appear (Hebrews 11:3). They came from the invisible.
2. First is the spiritual, and then comes the physical.
3. First is the thought and the meditation, and then comes the action and the manifestation!
4. For as he thinketh in his heart, so is he (Proverbs 23:7). Does this person become just because he had one little thought, or was it a continual and gradual process as he thought over and over, day in and day out? (You know the answer.)

Also, as individuals see themselves (because of how they think in their hearts), others see them in a similar manner. What is inside our hearts works as a projector for the world. It's a principle that the heart of a man reveals a man. And other people will ultimately see you as you really believe yourself to be.

> And there we saw the giants, the sons of Anak, which come of the giants: and we were in our own sight as grasshoppers, and so we were in their sight. (Numbers 13:33)

How do you see yourself? Do you see yourself as a grasshopper, or do you see yourself as a giant? How you see yourself is a choice, and you can choose today to begin seeing yourself as the child of God that you already are. What you are planting in your heart today will be revealed out in the open tomorrow. You will surely become the vision that you have planted in your heart.

Take some time and search within yourself and within your heart. God will show you (be ready to write it down; you wouldn't want to lose those life-changing revelations). He will meet you and speak to you IN YOUR HEART.

The child of God is special. He is a new creature, a supernatural species! Why or how? You belong to Him, and He bought you with the blood of His Son, Jesus. You're born anew of an incorruptible Seed, and you hold His Spirit.

> What? know ye not that your body is the temple of the Holy Ghost which is in you, which ye have of God, and ye are not your own? For ye are bought with a price: therefore glorify God in your body, and in your spirit, which are God's. (1 Corinthians 6:19–20)

You are the temple of God, and the Holy Spirit lives in your heart, and as your spirit searches within your heart, it comes and makes contact with the Holy Spirit, and the Holy Spirit is the Spirit of God and knows all things of God concerning you. Wouldn't you like to know what these heavenly things—these gifts—that God has freely given you are?

> But as it is written, Eye hath not seen, nor ear heard, neither have entered into the heart of man, the things which God hath prepared for them that love him. But God hath revealed them unto us by his Spirit: for the Spirit searcheth all things, yea, the deep things of God. For what man knoweth the things of a man, save the spirit of man which is in him? even so the things of God knoweth no man, but the Spirit of God. Now we have received, not the spirit of the world, but the spirit which is of God; **that we might know the things that are freely given to us of God**. (1 Corinthians 2:9–12, emphasis added)

God is waiting, the Holy Spirit is waiting, your gifts are waiting, and your vision is waiting. He is waiting for you to call. The Holy Bible says,

Call unto me, and I will answer thee, and shew thee
great and mighty things, which thou knowest not. (Jeremiah 33:3)

Jeremiah 29:12 says, "Then shall ye call upon me, and ye shall go
and pray unto me, and I will hearken unto you."

And ye shall seek me, and find me, when ye shall search
for me with all your heart. (Jeremiah 29:13)

When you meditate with all your heart, it's like playing and recit-
ing the things of God. It gets you in the Spirit, and like listening to a
song, it takes you to another place. When you commune with the Spirit,
you enter the realm of the unseen, and as you search, you will find. All
that you need is just one little glimpse from God, and it can change your
whole life and even the whole world—one snapshot, that's all. There's
infinite blessing inside you waiting to be liberated. "I call to remembrance my song in the night: I commune with mine own heart: and my
spirit made diligent search" (Psalm 77:6).

The world doesn't teach us about the heart, but the Holy Bible does.

As in water face answereth to face, so the heart of man
to man. (Proverbs 27:19)

It is our job to mine it out.

Counsel in the heart of man is like deep water; but a
man of understanding will draw it out. (Proverbs 20:5)

Saturate your heart with scripture reading and prayer. Worship Him
and fill yourself with the Spirit. Ask Him for a word, a sign, or a vision.

"The preparations of the heart in man, and the answer of the tongue, is from the LORD" (Proverbs 16:1).

The Holy Bible is a whole Book filled with His voice, which we can glean and incorporate from, in order to formulate a sure and compelling vision that we can securely stand on.

> My heart is overflowing with a good theme; I recite my
> composition concerning the King; my tongue is the pen
> of a ready writer. (Psalm 45:1 NKJV)

Prepare your heart by planting the Word inside of it. Get your heart's momentum going, warm up its engine, and see how it goes from your heart to your tongue, from the tongue to the page, and from the page to holding "it!" in your hands. Amen.

SOW THE VISION IN YOUR HEART

Then the LORD answered me and said: "Write the vision and make it plain on tablets, that he may run who reads it."

—Habakkuk 2:2 NKJV

_____

_____

_____

_____

_____

_____

_____

_____

_____

_____

_____

_____

_____

_____

_____

_____

_____

_____

_____

_____

_____

_____

CHAPTER 13

Sow Your Vision in Pain

There was a man in the Holy Bible whose name literally meant "he will cause pain." In those days, whatever your name was, that's what and who you were. All he knew was pain. He began in pain but was determined that he would not die in it. Though pain might have been a self-fulfilling prophecy, it wasn't God's prophecy for his life. Something inside him yearned, letting him know that he was created for much more. Perhaps, despite all his pain and the pain that he caused others, he had faith in God. And instead of all that pain making his heart as hard as stone, it made it soft and pliable. Hopeful?

> Now Jabez was more honorable than his brothers, and his mother called his name Jabez, saying, "Because I bore him in pain." And Jabez called on the God of Israel saying, "Oh, that You would bless me indeed, and enlarge my territory, that Your hand would be with me, and that You would keep me from evil, that I may not cause pain!" So God granted him what he requested. (1 Chronicles 4:9–10 NKJV)

This prayer made by Jabez stands out and comes out of nowhere. It is hidden and tucked away in between a long genealogy of names.

But he is singled out because he was different; he was more honorable than his brothers. Could it be that he wanted to change, and so he asked the only One Who could bring it about, and so God honored his vision? Jabez was able to visualize himself as "blessed indeed," a blessing that means that God's abundance overtakes and envelopes you, wrapping you up in a never-ending cycle. Like the waves crashing on the seashore, over and over again, crashing upon the rocks, splash! Blessings everywhere. Blessed indeed! Splash!

Heavenly Father, just like Jabez called upon You, so we, too, now pray "that You would enlarge our territory, our leadership, and our influence. Bless us so that we may bring glory to You, Your Son, and Your kingdom!"

You might be saying, "Not now. I'm barely hanging on by the last thread here." I've been there, and I've repeated those same words, but I shake it off! Like getting hit with freezing ice water. Backing out is not an option, so get back up and keep striking back! Continue to press forward. The reality is that there is nowhere else to go. Jesus holds the words of eternal life (John 6:68).

You may be in a battle, a struggle, or a dilemma. Perhaps you feel trapped, held back, confined, or even denied. I can somewhat relate to you. For I am writing these words from a prison cell. I've been here for thirteen and a half years. At the moment, my precious wife, Sandra, and my beautiful daughter, "Zoe" (going on three years old), are very ill because of COVID-19. And I'm waiting on the response to my court appeal in hopes that it gets granted so that I can go back, for the fourth time, to be resentenced. The judge will just not release me. (Not yet! The judge won't, but God will!) I feel like Moses when he kept on going before Pharaoh, the king of Egypt, saying,

> Thus saith the LORD, Let my people go, that they may serve me. (Exodus 8:1)

Only to be turned down, refused, and rejected. "But" God is in control, and He has a plan. Our God is the Judge of all judges. "But God is the judge: he putteth down one, and setteth up another" (Psalm 75:7).

The Hebrews, the children of God, were in bondage for 430 years! They were being used to make bricks so that the Egyptian empire could be expanded. Today, in modern times, many of us are still under bondage in various ways, and the bricks being made are no longer of straw and clay but of currency. So, what breaks the curse, the chains, and the yoke of bondage? The Holy Spirit! "It shall come to pass in that day That his burden will be taken away from your shoulder, And his yoke from your neck, And the yoke will be destroyed because of the anointing oil" (Isaiah 10:27 NKJV). Amen!

Possibly somebody or something is taking advantage of you unfairly because of how you look, how you sound, where you live, or where you come from. It can also be that, up to this point, you have been limited by the bad hand that life has dealt you. I have suffered and experienced this firsthand. But instead of focusing on it, I want to encourage you to cash in that hand for one that will bring you happiness, one that will give you peace, and one that will turn you into everything that you have always wanted to be!

> You have given him his heart's desire, and have not
> withheld the request of his lips.   SELAH
> For You meet him with the blessings of goodness; You
> set a crown of pure gold upon his head. (Psalm 21:2–3
> NKJV)

What do you have to lose? Write the vision and sow it in your heart.

Life is not easy, and not everything is a walk in the park. However, I can honestly look you in the eyes and tell you with all confidence, certainty, and assurance that "I am waiting on the vision," and "God is going to pull me out of here and hurl me into an atmosphere that's beyond anything that I can fathom." Is anything too hard for the LORD? Of course, not!

> Behold, the nations are as a drop of a bucket, and are counted as the small dust of the balance: behold, he ta-keth up the isles as a very little thing. (Isaiah 40:15)

I'm gently looking at you, and I ask, "What has you trapped?" or "What is hindering you?" Maybe it's neither, and you simply want something better for yourself, and there is nothing wrong with that. Whatever the challenge is, identify it and write your vision, above and beyond it, in agreement with the Word of God. You can then rest assured that the gates of hell will not prevail against you because you are not alone. You are joined, united, and banded—compacted and knit together—to a body of believers who have Christ Jesus as the head (Ephesians 4:16). The Spirit reminds us,

> No weapon that is formed against thee shall prosper; and every tongue that shall rise against thee in judgment thou shalt condemn. This is the heritage of the servants of the LORD, and their righteousness is of me, saith the LORD. (Isaiah 54:17)

Like Nehemiah, "RISE UP AND DECLARE!" that "no thing or things! Shall stand in my way nor in the way of the lives of those who I love," and "what shall we then say to these things? If God be for us, who can be against us?" (Romans 8:31).

RISE UP AND DECLARE! "Nay, in all these things we are more than conquerors through him that loved us" (Romans 8:37).

You are not fighting for yourselves, and you are not fighting alone. RISE UP AND DECLARE! "I can do all things through Christ which strengtheneth me" (Philippians 4:13). Now the still, small voice that spoke to the prophet Elijah when he was in a cave is whispering into your soul's ear right now,

> Ye are of God, little children, and have overcome them: because greater is he that is in you, than he that is in the world. (1 John 4:4)

Nothing can stand in our way.

> For whatsoever is born of God overcometh the world: and this is the victory that overcometh the world, even our faith. (1 John 5:4)

We win!
In pain or not, rain or shine, sow your vision anyway.

> They that sow in tears shall reap in joy. He that goeth forth and weepeth, bearing precious seed, shall doubt-less come again with rejoicing, bringing his sheaves with him. (Psalm 126:5–6)

God promises that those who sow in tears will reap in joy! He promises that if you go forth, sowing even in your tears, you will doubt-less, meaning "assuredly," return rejoicing, bringing your sheaves with you. The bundles, the heaps, and the mounts! Glory!

Sow Your Vision in Pain

Then the LORD answered me and said: "Write the vision and make it plain on tablets, that he may run who reads it."

—Habakkuk 2:2 NKJV

_____

_____

_____

_____

_____

_____

_____

_____

_____

_____

_____

_____

_____

_____

_____

_____

_____

_____

_____

_____

_____

_____

_____

YOUR VISION HAS POWER

Please, do not neglect the immeasurable capacity that lies dormant within you. I am here to tell you that you are reading this by divine appointment. God has an assignment for you.

On that night, ages ago, God told Abraham to look up at the stars and said,

> That in blessing I will bless thee, and in multiplying I
> will multiply thy seed as the stars of the heaven, and as
> the sand which is upon the sea shore; and thy seed shall
> possess the gate of his enemies. (Genesis 22:17)

The same God is inclining toward your direction and is telling you that He wants you to look at your hands, palms up (look down at them). They are empty, but He wants to fill them with all good things, just like He promised Abraham and much more. Now lift your hands a little bit higher. The great and awesome LORD wants to prepare them, for through these hands of yours, He wants to change the world!

> He teacheth my hands to war, so that a bow of steel is
> broken by mine arms. (Psalm 18:34)

You shall be a force to be reckoned with, and you will become mighty in the land. You shall do great exploits in Jesus's name!

> But ye shall receive power, after that the Holy Ghost is come upon you: and ye shall be witnesses unto me both in Jerusalem, and in all Judaea, and in Samaria, and unto the uttermost part of the earth. (Acts 1:8)

"You 'are' His secret weapon!"

> Thou art my battle axe and weapons of war: for with thee will I break in pieces the nations, and with thee will I destroy kingdoms; and with thee will I break in pieces the horse and his rider; and with thee will I break in pieces the chariot and his rider. (Jeremiah 51:20–21)

It's showtime!

> Arise, shine; for thy light is come, and the glory of the LORD is risen upon thee. (Isaiah 60:1)

Child of God, you can make a difference. "One man of you shall chase a thousand: for the LORD your God, he it is that fighteth for you, as he hath promised you" (Joshua 23:10).

Yes, one seed can break through concrete. I've seen it with my very own eyes. Why do you think that some sidewalks are all messed up? Once those seeds wake up (WAKE UP!) and begin growing, increasing, and developing, nothing can stop them as they strive upward to become!

Despite the opposition and resistance, on top of the untold pressure that's upon them, in the dark, they begin to push, PUSH, and PUSH! (Praying Until Something Happens)—until they crack in pieces and raise the concrete off the ground! It's a task that is a million times its size and weight. The destiny of the seed pulls it out because what the seed is to become is far too big to remain trapped. So great is the calling that not even concrete can hold it back. This is the type of force that your vision is going to produce and release. It's a force—a spiritual force with the capacity and capability to shake, to move, and even to revolutionize planet earth. Your life story, a powerful testimony, can go viral overnight!

When Jesus finished the parable of the soils, He said in conjunction,

> For there is nothing hid, which shall not be manifested; neither was any thing kept secret, but that it should come abroad. (Mark 4:22)

Nothing can stop your light from shining. It's the light of the Holy Spirit shining through you. Jesus said that we are the light of the world, right?

What our Master is also teaching us here is that similarly, though a seed is put under the ground, its purpose is not for it to remain hidden or concealed from view, but that it has to become exposed, made known, and displayed.

Jesus is also using these parables to describe and illustrate how His Word operates here on earth and how it works in the heart and life of a believer. "The sower soweth the word" (Mark 4:14). So I exhort you to sow the Word in your heart and to establish your vision on the same Word. This guarantees that He will bring it to pass.

There is nothing too big or too heavy that can hold you down because the Spirit of God that dwells in your heart is bigger. The light is His light, and it is brighter. The Word, the Seed, belongs to Him. The vision is His vision. And the power is His power!

> God hath spoken once; twice have I heard this; that power belongeth unto God. (Psalm 62:11)

> How should one chase a thousand, and two put ten
> thousand to flight. (Deuteronomy 32:30)

How can one chase a thousand? It's only through the power of God that dwells in your heart. You can preach to thousands, help and heal thousands, and bring them in by the thousands into the kingdom by the same power—the power that is in one name, and that is "Jesus!"

"We are weak, but ye are strong" (1 Corinthians 4:10). Jesus is our strength and power! Was that not the apostle Paul's secret weapon?

> For I determined not to know anything among you, save
> Jesus Christ, and him crucified. And I was with you in
> weakness, and in fear, and in much trembling. And my
> speech and my preaching was not with enticing words
> of man's wisdom, but in demonstration of the Spirit and
> of power: that your faith should not stand in the wisdom
> of men, but in the power of God. (1 Corinthians 2:2–5)

Take courage in God's gift, in the prophecies that have been made concerning you, and in your vision! What is God's gift? "The Spirit of power!"

> For God hath not given us the spirit of fear; but of pow-
> er, and of love, and of a sound mind. (2 Timothy 1:7)

YOUR VISION HAS POWER

Then the LORD answered me and said: "Write the vision and make it plain on tablets, that he may run who reads it."

—Habakkuk 2:2 NKJV

_____
_____
_____
_____
_____
_____
_____
_____
_____
_____
_____
_____
_____
_____
_____
_____
_____
_____
_____
_____
_____
_____
_____
_____

JESSE SUAREZ

CHAPTER 15

A VISION WITHOUT LIMITS

"Jesse, straight up. I'm becoming convinced, but tell me more. Tell me, why all the fuss about making the vision gigantic or without limits?"

I mean, you can make it as small or as big as you want. It's your choice and your life. However, pay close attention: "The Son of God," Jesus of Nazareth, the Messiah, God in the flesh, the second person of the Trinity, the only One Who can give everlasting Life, the One of Whose name the scripture says,

> Neither is there salvation in any other: for there is none other name under heaven given among men, whereby we must be saved. (Acts 4:12)

Yes, the same Jesus Who never sinned and Who never lied proclaimed,

> Heaven and earth shall pass away, but my words shall not pass away. (Matthew 24:35)

He also declared,

> For verily I say unto you, Till heaven and earth pass,
> one jot or one tittle shall in no wise pass from the law,
> till all be fulfilled. (Matthew 5:18)

This anointed Jesus, Who holds us in the palm of His hand, prophesied, stating,

> Verily, verily, I say unto you, He that believeth on me,
> the works that I do shall he do also; and greater works
> than these shall he do; because I go unto my Father.
> (John 14:12)

Jesus, Who walked on water without sinking, raised the dead, and fed thousands in one sitting, prophesied that you could do greater works! And for that to happen, you are going to need a big vision.

"Sons of the kingdom," I submit to you that this prophecy is yet to be fulfilled in its fullness because, personally, I don't see anywhere in the scripture where the apostles or disciples did greater works than Christ. We do see that His followers traveled farther, preaching the gospel for more years, and they reached more people. But evangelizing is one of the areas of ministry (extremely vital and important), one work, and Jesus said *works*—in plural form. They did do works, miracles, and some of the same ones that Christ did. By no means is that being discredited here. However, were they greater in magnitude?

I know that what is being presented may seem hard to take in, and some probably have stones in hand, thinking and mumbling, "What kind of new teaching is this?" It is not new, for Jesus said it and introduced it! Scripture also confirms all things and brings an end to all controversy. More than anything, scripture gives light and brings understanding.

We see in the Gospel of John, the same book that documents this prophecy, that the last verse in the last chapter ends with great insight pertaining to the works done by our Master. The Holy Bible says,

> And there are also many other things which Jesus did,
> the which, if they should be written every one, I sup-
> pose that even the world itself could not contain the
> books that should be written. Amen. (John 21:25)

The question posed is, "Who do you know in the Holy Bible or in the history of the church whose works were greater?" It hasn't happened, not *yet!*

Why did Jesus tell them this? Well, we first have to consider the circumstances and context of the setting. For it'll enhance the weight and significance of the narrative. His hour had arrived. It was an intense night, one filled with a lot of activity. Time was running out, and the lessons given to His disciples had not been completed. And His students were still grappling with trivial issues. For instance, Peter didn't want to get his feet washed. Thomas said, "We know not whither thou goest; and how can we know the way?" (John 14:5), all the while Judas (Iscariot) was lurking around, waiting for the opportune time to make a break for it, and slither away since he had his mind set on the thirty pieces of silver!

Yes, this was the night when Jesus's sweat became like great drops of blood. The same night in which He would be abandoned and denied, He would be carried away, arrested, and bound, headed to the cross.

In the midst of all that madness, Jesus had to take the time to inaugurate them since a transition was about to transpire, where He Himself was to usher in the rising of a new breed—the church (*ekklesia* in Greek, "an assembly"), the called out. The baton was about to be handed down to the next generation. The glistening Oil upon the head running down the beard was about to make "His" way to the whole body! (The Holy Spirit was about to hit the scene in a new way.)

This teacher-leader-to-student rite was a practice as old as the Old Testament. It also took place during transfers of blessings from father to son prior to the father's departure from the land of the living.

117

We see that Moses passed the leadership to his assistant, Joshua. Jacob blessed his twelve sons. King David handed the throne to his son Solomon. The apostle Paul also knew the value of this critical moment. He was aware that the time of his death was standing at the door. He had to transfer his ministry, so in haste, he wrote an epistle filled with all the love, vision, and authority of a spiritual father.

Imagine being Timothy, a young soldier, on the front line and reading the following:

> I charge thee therefore before God, and the Lord Jesus Christ, who shall judge the quick and the dead at his appearing and his kingdom; preach the word; be instant in season, out of season; reprove, rebuke, exhort with all longsuffering and doctrine. For the time will come when they will not endure sound doctrine; but after their own lusts shall they heap to themselves teachers, having itching ears; and they shall turn away their ears from the truth, and shall be turned unto fables. But watch thou in all things, endure afflictions, do the work of an evangelist, make full proof of thy ministry. For I am now ready to be offered, and the time of my departure is at hand. I have fought a good fight, I have finished my course, I have kept the faith: henceforth there is laid up for me a crown of righteousness, which the Lord, the righteous judge, shall give me at that day: and not to me only, but unto all them also that love his appearing. (2 Timothy 4:1–8)

This was the setting of that somber night, where every second counted.

It's impressive that the scripture makes a distinction between where Jesus was going and where the patriarchs went after they died. Abraham, Isaac, Jacob, Aaron, Moses, and King David "were gathered to their people, or gathered to their fathers" (Genesis 25:8, 35:29, 49:33; Deuteronomy 32:48–50; 1 Kings 2:10), as did all the other Old Testament saints.

In the Holy Bible, when it says, "Gathered to his people," it means they "joined their ancestors." However, Jesus never said that He was going to be gathered to His people, fathers, or ancestors. He said, "I came from the Father, and I'm returning to the Father" (returning to God).

> But now I go my way to him that sent me; and none of
> you asketh me, Whither goest thou? (John 16:5)

> These words spake Jesus, and lifted up his eyes to heaven, and said, Father, the hour is come; glorify thy Son, that thy Son also may glorify thee: as thou hast given him power over all flesh, that he should give eternal life to as many as thou hast given him. And this is life eternal, that they might know thee the only true God, and Jesus Christ, whom thou hast sent. I have glorified thee on the earth: I have finished the work which thou gavest me to do. And now, O Father, glorify thou me with thine own self with the glory which I had with thee before the world was. (John 17:1–5)

> I came forth from the Father, and am come into the world: again, I leave the world, and go to the Father. (John 16:28)

I love the following scripture. It's like the stone that slew Goliath. It's the scripture that confounds the babblers.

> In the beginning was the Word, and the Word was with
> God, and the Word was God. (John 1:1)

So what was Jesus conveying to all humanity by making these statements about returning to the Father?

Another question is, "Do you really know Who Jesus is?"

> Jesus Christ the same yesterday, and to day, and for ever. (Hebrews 13:8)

He doesn't change; therefore, since the Word was God and the Word is God, Jesus will always be God! "And the Word was made flesh, and dwelt among us, (and we beheld his glory, the glory as of the only begotten of the Father,) full of grace and truth" (John 1:14). The Word (God) became flesh (man), and as a perfect and sinless sacrifice, He died on the cross in our place. Therefore, our eternal salvation hinges upon this fact about who Jesus was and still is: "Christ the power of God, and the wisdom of God" (1 Corinthians 1:24).

> And without controversy great is the mystery of god-liness: God was manifest in the flesh, justified in the Spirit, seen of angels, preached unto the Gentiles, be-lieved on in the world, received up into glory. (1 Timothy 3:16)

Beloved, I beseech you to never waver from this eternal truth. Never falter because the biggest lie of the devil, false religions, and cults is to deny the Deity (godliness) of Jesus Christ. Jesus, being God, is where the power is. It is what sets us apart, and it is the confession of the true believer according to the Holy Bible. In 1 Timothy 3:16, we finished reading that "God was manifested in the flesh," which is talking about "the Word that became flesh" in John 1:14. (God, the Word, and Jesus are all One.)

It is written,

Hereby know ye the Spirit of God: Every spirit that con-
fesseth that Jesus Christ is come in the flesh is of God:
and every spirit that confessed not that Jesus Christ is
come in the flesh is not of God: and this is that spirit of
antichrist, whereof ye have heard that it should come;
and even now already is it in the world. (1 John 4:2–3)

Jesus urges us to "be not faithless, but believing" (John 20:27). As
He told doubting Thomas who turned into believing Thomas.

And Thomas answered and said unto him, **My Lord
and my God**. (John 20:28, emphasis added)

So where was Jesus returning? "God was returning back home."
Amen.

There He was, the Son of God, Who was "God the Son," about to
be delivered, and He was concerned with the state and the spiritual wel-
fare of His disciples. He reassured His little flock that they were going to
be fine and that He would not leave them orphans. He encouraged them
by conveying to them that where He left off, they would continue to the
point of doing even greater signs, works, and wonders. In a sense, Jesus
was transferring His earthly vision to them. Wow!

How would it be possible for them to do more than the Master,
though? Well, what does the Word say? Let's delve in together. Let's
break it down and unpack it.

For now, this shall be our foundational scripture:

Verily, verily, I say unto you, He that believeth on me,
the works that I do shall he do also and greater works
than these shall he do; because I go unto my Father.
(John 14:12)

This prophecy tells us a few things.

1. We must believe in Jesus.
2. The statement "He that believeth" is an open invitation for "whosoever" and to all nations until He returns.
3. We would do greater works than Jesus.
4. Because Jesus was going to the Father, this would be made possible.

I believe that this part of the prophecy will give us perspective on the way in which we have always viewed it. Let's do some deeper expounding.

In John 14:10, Jesus makes it clear:

But the Father that dwelleth in me, he doeth the works.

Okay, this one is easy to understand: "That the Father was inside of Christ doing the works."

So "how was the Father in Christ?" Oh, that's another easy one. It was through the Holy Spirit. Remember when He was baptized and the Holy Spirit fell upon Him in bodily form, like a dove? (Luke 3:22). "Yes, that's true. I do recall that John the Baptist baptized Him."

Jesus also said that the Father was greater (John 14:28). And that once He was with the Father, then the same Spirit that was inside of Him, Who did the miracles, would be inside them. That's the same Holy Spirit that is also inside of us today.

"That's a bold statement. How can you be 100 percent sure that we are talking about the same Spirit here, Jesse?"

"Because the Holy Bible tells us. That's why (How do we know that Jesus loves us? Yes! Because the Bible tells us so)."

The Holy Bible says,

> But if the Spirit of him that raised up Jesus from the
> dead dwell in you, he that raised up Christ from the
> dead shall also quicken your mortal bodies by his Spirit
> that dwelleth in you. (Romans 8:11)

It would be this same Holy Spirit that would hence be able to perform the greater works through the believer.

Now the works done through the hands and words of Christ when He walked the earth were one thing, but Jesus made them twofold. He made it possible for us to receive a "double whammy!" (Man! That's why I love Him! He's so good!) Because, pay attention, "the works that I do shall he do also." That's one part. Boom! "And greater works than these shall he do." That's the second part. Boom! Boom! (Do you see it, too, or am I tripping?)

5.   The believer must ask the Father, in the name of Jesus. "And whatsoever ye shall ask in my name, that will I do, that the Father may be glorified in the Son. If ye shall ask anything in my name, I will do it" (John 14:13–14).

There's a saying, and though I've never liked it, there's truth to it. It goes, "Closed mouth don't get fed."

> And **whatever things** you ask in prayer, believing, you
> will receive. (Matthew 21:22 NKJV, emphasis added)

The above scripture we just read from Matthew sums up the two previous verses from the book of John through the statement of "whatever things."

> And whatsoever ye shall ask in my name, that will I do,
> that the Father may be glorified in the Son. (John 14:13)

If ye shall ask any thing in my name, I will do it. (John 14:14)

"Whatever things" (whatsoever and anything)—these two words literally unbridle the size, volume, and magnitude of what we can ask for. We are to ask for "whatever" unlimited and for "anything" unlimited.

Nothing is too small, nor is anything too big for God. He is the source! He can never run out, and He doesn't have a poverty mentality—a poverty, log cabin mindset. The only things that can limit Him are the limits that we place on Him at the levels and degrees of our asking. Big vision, big asking. Little vision, little asking. He is the Almighty, as in all limitless!

6.   We must love Jesus and be obedient to the Word. "If ye love me, keep my commandments" (John 14:15).

I know that all of this sounds surreal, but it's true. It's in the Holy Bible. This is a prophecy that was spoken by Jesus, and there is a reason this has come to your attention, and it is that God is calling you for such a time as this—a time in which you shall do "the greater works than these!"

For Jesus said,

Ye have not chosen me, but I have chosen you, and ordained you, that ye should go and bring forth fruit, and that your fruit should remain: that whatsoever ye shall ask of the Father in my name, he may give it you. (John 15:16)

A VISION WITHOUT LIMITS

Then the LORD answered me and said: "Write the vision and make it plain on tablets, that he may run who reads it."

—Habakkuk 2:2 NKJV

_____

_____

_____

_____

_____

_____

_____

_____

_____

_____

_____

_____

_____

_____

_____

_____

_____

_____

_____

_____

_____

_____

_____

_____

THE LITTLE SEED

THE VISION OF DOUBLE PORTION

Excuse us, instructor, "not the same works, but the greater works, would you like to explain?" It's not what I can tell you that matters; it's "what-does-the-Word-say?"

Jesus said it, and since He did, it's true, and it must come to pass. He also used the terms *verily, verily,* which is to say "most assuredly." I mean, how or who can question that? We are not trying to do that here. I know, but it's just hard to ingest and process, right?

"Yes, 'that part.'"

Okay, let's get into it. "Let's go!" Let's do some expository work. Off the top, we see that there was something beyond our comprehension about Jesus going away and being united with the Father, which was going to cause the anointing to be amplified as the Holy Spirit was to be poured out. This specific act of the Holy Spirit being poured out was also a prophecy, one that had long been awaited. It had echoed from generation to generation.

> And it shall come to pass afterward, that I will pour out
> my spirit upon all flesh; and your sons and your daugh-
> ters shall prophesy, your old men shall dream dreams, your
> young men shall see visions: and also upon the servants

and upon the handmaids in those days will I pour out
my spirit. (Joel 2:28–29)

During this instance, as Jesus was speaking to His disciples, the
Spirit of God did not live in them yet, for He said,

And I will pray the Father, and he shall give you another Comforter, that he may abide with you for ever;
even the Spirit of truth; whom the world cannot receive,
because it seeth him not, neither knoweth him: but ye
know him; **for he dwelleth with you, and shall be in
you**. (John 14:16–17, emphasis added)

They were familiar with the Holy Spirit. He dwelt with them but
was not inside of them. That would come later.

Let's direct our attention to what Christ said concerning the Holy
Spirit. We already covered where He said, "But the Father that dwelleth
in me, he doeth the works." He further says,

If a man love me, he will keep my words: and my Father
will love him, and **we** will come unto him, and make
our abode with him. (John 14:23, emphasis added)

Did you catch that? Jesus said, "'We' will come unto him, and
make our abode with him." That means "in" him. Glory! Once the believer receives the indwelling of the Holy Spirit, he or she also becomes
inhabited by the Father and the Son. For in Christ, we get the whole
package.

For in him dwelleth all the fulness of the Godhead bodily. And ye are complete in him, which is the head of all
principality and power. (Colossians 2:9–10)

Therefore, do not root, establish, or build your "vision" upon any-one else, for there is nothing out there or anywhere else to turn to where we can receive power and have good success.

Jesus told us,

> I am the vine, ye are the branches: He that abideth in
> me, and I in him, the same bringeth forth much fruit: for
> without me ye can do nothing. (John 15:5)

We, as believers, become endued with power from on high to do incredible things, but we must never forget that we are merely conduits.

> But we have this treasure in earthen vessels, that the
> excellency of the power may be of God, and not of us.
> (2 Corinthians 4:7)

It is not "us"; it can never be of us. It's "ALL" about Him!

Okay, "now I get it. I think?" Jesus said, "The Father that dwelleth in me, he doeth the works, so Jesus came to earth to teach us, by being an example, into the dynamics of a relationship between God and mankind. As the scripture reminds us,"

> Let this mind be in you, which was also in Christ Jesus:
> who, being in the form of God, thought it not robbery to
> be equal with God: but made himself of no reputation,
> and took upon him the form of a servant, and was made
> in the likeness of men: and being found in fashion as a
> man, he humbled himself, and became obedient unto
> death, even the death of the cross. (Philippians 2:5–8)

> How God anointed Jesus of Nazareth with the Holy
> Ghost and with power: who went about doing good, and

healing all that were oppressed of the devil; for God was with him. (Acts 10:38)

Absolutely! "You got it. Good job!" Let's keep going.

Our Heavenly Father knew that His Son would one day come to earth and that He would duplicate Himself in us by equipping us with His Word, training, and by filling us with the Holy Spirit. So once Jesus had reconciled us back to the Father and duplicated Himself in us, then as Jesus did with us and for us, through the same power, we would "in His name" and as His representatives do the same for others.

> And all things are of God, who hath reconciled us to himself by Jesus Christ, and hath given to us the ministry of reconciliation; to wit, that God was in Christ, reconciling the world unto himself, not imputing their trespasses unto them; and hath committed unto us the word of reconciliation. Now then we are ambassadors for Christ, as though God did beseech you by us: we pray you in Christ's stead, be ye reconciled to God. (2 Corinthians 5:18–20)

We are His ambassadors!

Thirteen years ago, I was in the Los Angeles County Men's Central Jail. I was still fighting my case. An older woman went to the jail to preach and teach the Word. I could tell that she was nervous and new to sharing the gospel. (Why she was there wasn't of her, though. It was of the Holy Spirit.) She was the first person who ever told me that I was an ambassador for Christ. She planted the seed, and I never forgot, and I will never forget that moment.

Child of God, wherever you are, whatever country you live in, whether you are in jail, in prison, in a hotel, in the back of an alley, or whether you are living on top of the hill, Jesus loves YOU, and you are the right person for the assignment.

Give it time. You'll see.

This is His plan. If somebody doesn't like it, they can take it up with Him. I love it myself. I mean, you can't lose. This is the winning team!

Jesus is "the firstborn among many brethren" (Romans 8:29). Many, many brethren would follow in His footsteps. As we get adopted into the family of God, we receive everlasting life, and He also births in us a vision to live out while here on earth—a vision that is beyond our wildest dreams!

> Behold ye among the heathen [nations], and regard, and wonder marvellously: for I will work a work in your days, which ye will not believe, though it be told you. (Habakkuk 1:5)

Trust me. Whatever you are going through, our Heavenly Father can turn it around for you with the snap of His finger. SNAP!

Hold on. It gets better.

This great declaration of "the works that I do shall he do also; and greater works than these shall he do" was nothing new in the scripture. It had happened before in a similar setting. I wonder if the passage of Elijah, when he was taken to heaven, resonated in anyone's heart that night. During that episode, the prophet Elijah was going to be taken away by God, and his disciple "Elisha" would not stop following him. And Elijah, prior to leaving, wanted his spiritual son to be prepared for his journey. So he imparted upon him a spiritual gift (sound familiar?).

> And it came to pass, when they were gone over, that Elijah said unto Elisha, Ask what I shall do for thee, before I be taken away from thee. And Elisha said, I pray thee, let a **double portion** of thy spirit be upon me. And he said, Thou hast asked a hard thing: nevertheless, if thou see me when I am taken from thee, it shall be so

131

unto thee; but if not, it shall not be so. And it came to pass, as they still went on, and talked, that, behold, there appeared a chariot of fire, and horses of fire, and parted them both asunder; and Elijah went up by a whirlwind into heaven. And Elisha saw it, and he cried, My father, my father, the chariot of Israel, and the horsemen thereof. And he saw him no more: and he took hold of his own clothes, and rent them in two pieces. He took up also the mantle of Elijah that fell from him, and went back, and stood by the bank of Jordan; and he took the mantle of Elijah that fell from him, and smote the waters, and said, Where is the LORD God of Elijah? and when he also had smitten the waters, they parted hither and thither: and Elisha went over. (2 Kings 2:9–14, emphasis added)

We see here that the master goes away but leaves behind a double portion of his spirit for his disciple. We also see that Elisha wasted no time; he instantly performed a miracle by calling upon the God of Elijah. He split the waters of Jordan!

It's worth noting that these two prophets also raised the dead and did many other remarkable miracles.

The prophet Elijah was heavy-duty; there's no doubting that. Let us not fail to recall "the big showdown on Mount Carmel," when he stood by himself against and defeated the four hundred and fifty prophets of Baal (1 Kings 18:22, 40). That was the day when he called down fire from heaven! (Revealing to all saints and foes, down the corridors of time, how God can use one man... Child of God, those hands of yours, those are His weapons. Your lips, those are the floodgates through which God wants to bless the world. You are of great value to Him.)

And yet his prodigy, with all clarity of mind, boldness, and faith, asks for a double portion of his master's spirit—of his anointing. One of the evident reasons for this audacious request was that Elisha had a bigger vision! This young man had visualized, imagined, and pictured himself doing greater works for the glory of the God whom he served.

This audacious request was deliberate, intentional, and calculated. Elisha's eyes have been opened; he has been exposed to the power of God, working through man! His teacher did miracles, and he had witnessed them firsthand, and now he wanted to continue where Elijah left off.

I wonder how many nights Elisha meditated on his bed or as he slept under the open sky, imagining within his heart, saying to himself, "One day, I will be like my master Elijah, and the works that he does I will do, and even greater works than those."

Elisha was able to receive a "double portion" of Elijah's spirit because he asked, and he was only able to ask according to what he had already stored in his heart. In other words, he already had a seed planted. A baby was already growing inside his spiritual womb. "For out of the abundance of the heart the mouth speaketh" (Matthew 12:34). He wasn't caught slippin' or sleeping.

This request was also in line with the will of the LORD. Today, Jesus Christ believes and anticipates that we can do "the same" and "even greater works" than He did by the same will of the same God.

Since the spiritual principle of the "double portion" is written and established by scripture, it already has the approval of headquarters. All that you have to do is make the call (and He will answer you!).

This is power! What you are learning is the Holy Bible!

If Jesus Christ said to you right now, "Ask what I may do for you," would you have it within you to respond with, "The works that You did, I want to do, and greater works than those also"? How would you answer Him? Through His Word and His Spirit, He is asking you that question right now.

How much are you really hoping for?

> As for thee also, by the blood of thy covenant I have sent
> forth thy prisoners out of the pit wherein is no water.

Turn you to the strong hold, ye prisoners of hope: even
to day do I declare **I will render double unto thee**.
(Zechariah 9:11–12, emphasis added)

It is not a hard thing for God to give us double.

Instead of your shame you shall have double honor, and
instead of confusion they shall rejoice in their portion.
Therefore in their land they shall possess double; everlasting joy shall be theirs. (Isaiah 61:7 NKJV)

Before we move forward, I want us to focus on another similarity.
It's a little one, but it's worth mentioning. Elijah said to Elisha,

Ask what I shall do for thee, before I be taken away
from thee. (2 Kings 2:9)

And Jesus said to His disciples,

And whatsoever ye shall ask in my name, that will I do.
(John 14:13)

Elijah didn't guarantee anything. He said, "Thou hast asked a hard
thing: Nevertheless, if thou see me when I am taken from thee, it shall
be so unto thee; but if not, it shall not be so" (2 Kings 2:10). Jesus, the
Messiah, on the other hand, certifies it. He says "whatsoever" and "anything" you ask, I will do it (John 14:13–14). (So long as it brings glory
to the Father.)

Elisha, a servant, asked, and we servants of the Most High God
shall ask as well!

> Ask, and it shall be given you; seek, and ye shall find; knock, and it shall be opened unto you: for every one that asketh receiveth; and he that seeketh findeth; and to him that knocketh it shall be opened. (Matthew 7:7–8)

God wants to use us, and He will. However, we must start getting into the habit of asking in a more precise manner. Elisha was direct. He said, "I want a double portion of your spirit." Bam! Period. He wasn't wishy-washy.

If we don't have a vision centered on Christ, we won't even know where to start or how to ask. There's a scripture that speaks about this, saying, "Ye have not, because ye ask not" (James 4:2).

> You ask and do not receive, because you ask amiss, that you may spend it on your pleasures. (James 4:3 NKJV)

If Jesus said that we can ask for "whatever" and for "anything" and it will be done, then that's what it is. There are no *ifs*, *ands*, or *buts* about it.

Let's be honest, though. Who do the majority of people usually ask for? "Am I asking for myself and my pleasures, or am I asking on behalf of the church, the kingdom of God, or His flock?" For whose good pleasure?

I don't see anywhere in the Scripture where Jesus did a miracle for Himself. It's not in the Book.

Don't get me wrong. We are a blessed people. But we are blessed for a purpose. The following is a blessing that was given to Abraham—a blessing that was transferred to us through Jesus Christ. Do you really know how blessed you are already?

The following are the blessings of God given to Abraham:

135

> And I will make of thee a great nation, and I will bless
> thee, and make thy name great; and thou shalt be a
> blessing. (Genesis 12:2)

Our wonderful Lord and Savior took upon Himself the penalty of sin, which was death. For while we were still sinners, He loved us, died for us, and blessed us on top of it all. "For the wages of sin is death; but the gift of God is eternal life through Jesus Christ our Lord" (Romans 6:23). And our wages were paid by Him by dying on the cross. Because of His sacrifice, we can now receive everlasting life, the Holy Spirit, and blessings.

The Holy Bible says,

> Christ hath redeemed us from the curse of the law, being
> made a curse for us: for it is written, Cursed is every one
> that hangeth on a tree: **that the blessing of Abraham**
> **might come on the Gentiles through Jesus Christ**;
> that we might receive the promise of the Spirit through
> faith. (Galatians 3:13–14, emphasis added)

> There is neither Jew nor Greek, there is neither bond
> nor free, there is neither male nor female: for ye are
> all one in Christ Jesus. And if ye be Christ's then are
> ye Abraham's seed, and heirs according to the promise.
> (Galatians 3:28–29)

It doesn't matter who you are or where you came from. If you are a believer in Jesus Christ, the blessings of Abraham belong to you too! Here are just a few blessings from the book of Deuteronomy:

> And all these blessings shall come on thee, and over-
> take thee, if thou shalt hearken unto the voice of the

LORD thy God. Blessed shalt thou be in the city, and blessed shalt thou be in the field. Blessed shall be the fruit of thy body, and the fruit of thy ground, and the fruit of thy cattle, the increase of thy kine, and the flocks of thy sheep. Blessed shall be thy basket and thy store. Blessed shalt thou be when thou comest in, and blessed shalt thou be when thou goest out. The LORD shall cause thine enemies that rise up against thee to be smitten before thy face: they shall come out against thee one way, and flee before thee seven ways. The LORD shall command the blessing upon thee in thy storehouses, and in all that thou settest thine hand unto; and he shall bless thee in the land which the LORD thy God giveth thee. The LORD shall establish thee an holy people unto himself, as he hath sworn unto thee, if thou shalt keep the commandments of the LORD thy God, and walk in his ways. And all people of the earth shall see that thou art called by the name of the LORD; and they shall be afraid of thee. And the LORD shall make thee plenteous in goods, in the fruit of thy body, and in the fruit of thy cattle, and in the fruit of thy ground, in the land which the LORD sware unto thy fathers to give thee. The LORD shall open unto thee his good treasure, the heaven to give the rain unto thy land in his season, and to bless all the work of thine hand: and thou shalt lend unto many nations, and thou shalt not borrow. And the LORD shall make thee the head, and not the tail; and thou shalt be above only, and thou shalt not be beneath; if that thou hearken unto the commandments of the LORD thy God, which I command thee this day, to observe and to do them: And thou shalt not go aside from any of the words which I command thee this day,

to the right hand, or to the left, to go after other gods to
serve them. (Deuteronomy 28:2–14)

Verse 1 of Deuteronomy 28 says, "And it shall come to pass, if thou
shalt hearken diligently unto the voice of the LORD thy God, to observe
and to do all his commandments which I command thee this day, that
the LORD thy God will set thee on high above all nations of the earth."

God will set us high above all the nations of the earth, but how shall
we use our influence to make disciples of all nations? Why do we want
miracles? What do we plan on doing with the blessings? What is our
primary motivation? What is the spirit behind it all?

Again, if it's not in our hearts, we won't be able to envision it, and
if we can't envision it, then we won't ask for it. A vision of a double
portion requires a person with a heart that will do double the asking. "If
thou canst believe, all things are possible to him that believeth" (Mark
9:23). Jesus said that!

THE VISION OF DOUBLE PORTION

Then the LORD answered me and said: "Write the vision and make it plain on tablets, that he may run who reads it."

—Habakkuk 2:2 NKJV

_____

_____

_____

_____

_____

_____

_____

_____

_____

_____

_____

_____

_____

_____

_____

_____

_____

_____

_____

_____

_____

_____

_____

_____

_____

CHAPTER 17

THE VISION OF THE GOOD AND FAITHFUL SERVANT

On the twenty-seventh day of February, in the year 2022, at 5:00 a.m., the Word of the LORD came to me and said, "Shepherds are like bankers." The Word was straight to the point.

I began meditating. "How are shepherds like bankers?" and then I went to the Holy Bible to get the answers. I also asked myself, "What does a banker do?" and I came up with some light answers. They are to protect the public's currency, valuables, assets, and the like. And if a person has funds in their account and they request a withdrawal, it is the banker's job to release that money. A banker can also give out loans. The wealth does not belong to the bankers; they are merely stewards. They are also to increase the people's wealth.

In like manner, the shepherds are to protect, care for, and defend the flock, which are God's children. They are also to increase them by teaching, equipping, and multiplying them in the knowledge and wisdom of the things of God. Shepherds are the leaders; therefore, they are to be good examples of how to live a victorious life and how to make it happen the "overcomer" Christian way!

> Feed the flock of God which is among you, taking the
> oversight thereof, not by constraint, but willingly; not

141

for filthy lucre, but of a ready mind; neither as being lords over God's heritage, but being ensamples to the flock. And when the chief Shepherd shall appear, ye shall receive a crown of glory that fadeth not away. (1 Peter 5:2–4)

The shepherds equip the Christians, and they then go out into the world to do the work of the ministry. The flock comes to the church, receives their instructions, and gets to work for the kingdom. They get their tanks filled with vision, and they run with it!

And he gave some, apostles; and some, prophets; and some, evangelists; and some, pastors and teachers; for the perfecting of the saints, for the work of the ministry, for the edifying of the body of Christ. (Ephesians 4:11–12)

The objective is to edify and strengthen the flock, not to focus on shaking them down for their gold, silver, or shekels. People are God's greatest jewels (Malachi 3:17). He takes His children very seriously.

In the following parable, God uses servants and money to illustrate how He deals with and feels in regard to His kingdom.

The parable of the talents:

For the kingdom of heaven is as a man travelling into a far country, who called his own servants, and delivered unto them his goods. And unto one he gave five talents, to another two, and to another one; to every man according to his several ability; and straightway took his journey. Then he that had received the five talents went and traded with the same, and made them other five talents. And likewise he that had received two, he also gained other two. But he that had received one

142

went and digged in the earth, and hid his lord's money. After a long time the lord of hose servants cometh, and reckoneth with them. And so he that had received five talents came and brought other five talents, saying, Lord, thou deliveredst unto me five talents: behold, I have gained beside them five talents more. His lord said unto him, Well done, thou good and faithful servant: thou hast been faithful over a few things, I will make thee ruler over many things: enter thou into the joy of thy lord. He also that had received two talents came and said, Lord, thou deliveredst unto me two talents: behold, I have gained two other talents beside them. His lord said unto him, Well done, good and faithful servant; thou hast been faithful over a few things, I will make thee ruler over many things: enter thou into the joy of thy lord. Then he which had received the one talent came and said, Lord, I knew thee that thou art an hard man, reaping where thou hast not sown, and gathering where thou hast not strawed: and I was afraid, and went and hid thy talent in the earth: lo, there thou hast that is thine. His lord aswered and said unto him, Thou wicked and slothful servant, thou knewest that I reap where I sowed not, and gather where I have not strawed: thou oughtest therefore to have put my money to the exchangers [bankers], and then at my coming I should have received mine own with usury [interest]. Take therefore the talent from him, and give it unto him which hath ten talents. (Matthew 25:14–28)

One of God's names is "Jehovah-Jireh" (Genesis 22:14), which means "the LORD will provide." Our God will provide as He always has and does. He will also hold us accountable for every soul placed in our care.

143

What about you? Have you sincerely trusted in Him and given Him a try?

> Let us therefore come boldly unto the throne of grace,
> that we may obtain mercy, and find grace to help in time
> of need. (Hebrews 4:16)

Can it be that some shepherds act wrongfully because they are unaware of what has been made available to them by the blood of Christ? Perhaps they have a small vision, or, as the parable pointed out, the servant was lazy. Whatever the case may be, God wants His shepherds today to turn back to Him and His Word.

> But thou shalt remember the LORD thy God: for it is he
> that giveth thee power to get wealth, that he may establish his covenant which he sware unto thy fathers, as it
> is this day. (Deuteronomy 8:18)

I'm telling you, get sold out for Jesus, push all your chips in, and you will see that with Him you can't lose.

This is what Jesus said concerning those who follow Him:

> And Jesus answered and said, Verily I say unto you,
> There is no man that hath left house, or brethren, or sisters, or father, or mother, or wife, or children, or lands,
> for my sake, and the gospel's, but he shall receive an
> hundredfold now in this time, houses, and brethren, and
> sisters, and mothers, and children, and lands, with persecutions; and in the world to come eternal life. (Mark
> 10:29–30)

The apostle Paul reminded the Corinthian church, saying, "Now ye are full, now ye are rich, ye have reigned as kings without us" (1 Corinthians 4:8). He was telling them that they were already full and that they were already rich! Imagine someone running around, begging, and stealing bread because they don't know that they are already rich? No vision (sad face).

He is our source! He knows what we need, and He died so that we could have it. The apostle Paul couldn't make it any simpler:

> For ye know the grace of our Lord Jesus Christ, that, though he was rich, yet for your sakes he became poor, that ye through his poverty might be rich. (2 Corinthians 8:9)

This next scripture is one that I have hidden in my heart.

> The blessing of the LORD, it maketh rich, and he addeth no sorrow with it. (Proverbs 10:22)

Sometimes we tend to forget that our Heavenly Father owns it all.

> The silver is mine, and the gold is mine, saith the LORD of hosts. (Haggai 2:8)

Everything is His. "The cattle upon a thousand hills" (Psalm 50:10) belongs to Him! So it's only a matter of asking. As long as we seek Him and put Him first, everything will fall into place.

> But seek ye first the kingdom of God, and his righteousness; and all these things shall be added unto you. (Matthew 6:33)

Don't chase the denarii, *el dinero*, or the dollars. Chase the Master, and everything else will chase you, "indeed." As it says in Psalm 23, "Surely goodness and mercy shall follow me all the days of my life: and I will dwell in the house of the LORD for ever" (Psalm 23:6). The blessings will be so great and so much that there will not be enough room to receive them (Malachi 3:10). You'll have no choice but to give it away and be a blessing!

Here, we see Jesus correcting one of His shepherds in love.

> He saith unto him the third time, Simon, son of Jonas, lovest thou me? Peter was grieved because he said unto him the third time, Lovest thou me? And he said unto him, Lord, thou knowest all things; thou knowest that I love thee. Jesus saith unto him, Feed my sheep. (John 21:17)

What about us? "Do we love Him?" Then let's feed His sheep. Let's get to work!

YOU. I'm going to ask.
ME.   Go ahead. He's been waiting.
YOU. Father God, in the mighty name of Jesus, I ask You to fill me with the power of the Holy Spirit and send me all over the world so that I may proclaim Your gospel, beginning at my home, then in my neighborhood, and finally abroad if that be Your will for me, so that I may save souls for Your glory! In accordance with what Jesus has commissioned me to do.

> Go ye therefore, and teach all nations, baptizing them in the name of the Father, and of the Son, and of the Holy Ghost: teaching them to observe all things whatsoever I have commanded you: and, lo, I am with you

always, even unto the end of the world. Amen. (Matthew 28:19–20)

YOU. Like that?

ME. That's beautiful! Now write it on a flashcard, notebook, or your smartphone, somewhere where you can readily access it. Then read it to yourself over and over every day, preferably audibly. That's meditation the Holy Bible way. Begin imagining or visualizing the scripture being fulfilled in your life. Also, start taking action steps, even if they are small, and build from there. Good job, though. Prayers like this one will lead you to set the world ablaze.

Meditating on the Word of God is part of being a good and faithful servant and steward. I mean, how will we be able to occupy and do business until He returns? (Luke 19:13). It's crucial! Sons of the kingdom, meditating on the Word is one of the strongest weapons and tools in our arsenal. Meditation keeps a constant line of communication open between you and God.

It also keeps us blessed!

> Blessed is the man that walketh not in the counsel of the
> ungodly, nor standeth in the way of sinners, nor sitteth
> in the seat of the scornful. But his delight is in the law
> of the LORD; and in his law doth he meditate day and
> night. And he shall be like a tree planted by the rivers of
> water, that bringeth forth his fruit in his season; his leaf
> also shall not wither; and whatsoever he doeth shall
> prosper. (Psalm 1:1–3)

Because he meditates on the Word of God day and night, he is a fruitful and prosperous tree whose roots go down into the deep waters of the Holy Spirit. Therefore, he shall be successful in all his (or her) endeavors in the furtherance of the kingdom. And thus, we will be able to lead His flock well.

> This book of the law shall not depart out of thy mouth; but thou shalt meditate therein day and night, that thou mayest observe to do according to all that is written therein: for then thou shalt make thy way prosperous, and then thou shalt have good success. (Joshua 1:8)

Meditate so that you will observe and do all that is written in the Holy Book. When we meditate, we observe the scripture with the intention of doing for ourselves everything that is in there. In our hearts, we march where they marched, and we do what they did. It is then that this Book comes alive and begins speaking, letting us know that the things that they went through and the things that happened to them were examples, and they were written for our edification and encouragement. It is this Book that tells us who we are; it tells us what we can do and reveals to us what we can have and, most importantly, "how to use it all for His glory." Meditation allows the spiritual roots of our hearts to drink from the rivers and channels of God's love, power, knowledge, and understanding through the Holy Spirit.

This is an intimate inner process that produces outer and public results. Observe what to do on the inside in the simulator of the heart, and then and only then will you make your way prosperous, and then you will have good success on the outside.

On the inside, it's meditation, imagination, and simulation, which equate to the Word being conceived and concealed! In Hebrews 4:2, we are taught that if we want the Word of God to be profitable to us, we have to mix it with faith. Then on the outside, after we make preparation and take action, it becomes the Word exposed, revealed, and manifested!

Remember the servants (stewards) who were given the talents in the parable? If you recall, the master didn't tell them how to increase their talents. That was their job. The two who did increase did so because they used their "creativity." In other words, they used their "imaginations." What you are about to learn next is another game changer if you apply it.

In the following two scriptures, the words *meditate* and *imagine* mean the same thing.

> But his delight is in the law of the LORD; and in his law doth he **meditate** day and night. (Psalm 1:2, emphasis added)

> Why do the heathen rage, and the people **imagine** a vain thing? (Psalm 2:1, emphasis added)

When we meditate, we have to use our imagination. And this is important because it is in our minds, in the imagination of the heart, where the Word of God is conceived; it's where CONCEPTION takes place.

In the following two scriptures, the words *mind* and *imagination* have the same Hebrew meaning. It is the Hebrew word "***yetser***," and it means "**conception**."

> Thou wilt keep him in perfect peace, whose **mind** is stayed on thee: because he trusteth in thee. (Isaiah 26:3, emphasis added)

> And God saw that the wickedness of man was great in the earth, and that every **imagination** of the thoughts of his heart was only evil continually. (Genesis 6:5, emphasis added)

What does this mean? It means that if we can conceive the scriptures with the mind and the imagination of the heart, then God will be able to give birth to them. What we meditate on in our hearts today will be the life that we will be living out tomorrow. Shepherds, what is the vision for you and your flock, and how big is it?

There is nowhere in the Holy Bible where we are told to conceive little; in fact, we are encouraged to believe and to give conception to miracles, to move mountains, to heal the sick, to raise the dead, and even to call fire down from heaven! Shepherds, let's stretch our vision! If the Word says we can do it, then we can do it. According to God's Word, we just have to conceive it first. Use your "*yetser*," your imagination, to believe that you have already received it. It's already done!

Jesus is the one teaching us here, saying,

> For verily I say unto you, That whosoever shall say unto this mountain, Be thou removed, and be thou cast into the sea; and shall not doubt in his heart, but shall believe that those things which he saith shall come to pass; he shall have whatsoever he saith. Therefore I say unto you, What things soever ye desire, when ye pray, **believe that ye receive them**, and ye shall have them. (Mark 11:23–24, emphasis added)

Don't doubt with your heart, but believe and meditate within your heart because you will never be able to believe that you have received something without using the "*yetser*," the imagination of your heart. Psalm 19:14 says, "Let the words of my mouth, and the meditation of my heart, be acceptable in thy sight, O LORD, my strength, and my redeemer."

When we meditate on His Word, it builds our faith. "So then faith cometh by hearing, and hearing by the word of God" (Romans 10:17). It is in our constant hearing of His Word that increases our faith, and faith is what causes God to move.

> He therefore that ministereth to you the Spirit, and wor-
> keth miracles among you, doeth he it by the works of
> the law, or by the hearing of faith? (Galatians 3:5)

All of us desire to hear, "Well done, thou good and faithful servant: thou hast been faithful over a few things, I will make thee ruler over many things: enter thou into the joy of thy lord" (Matthew 25:21). And then He will commit to our trust the true riches (Luke 16:11). Amen to that!

YOU. Why didn't you finish the parable of the talents?

ME. The last two verses were a little harsh.

YOU. The shepherds need to know so that they may be without excuse on the day of judgment.

ME. True that, thou hast said rightly.

We will continue from where we left off in the last verse. The scripture says,

> Take therefore the talent from him, and give it unto him
> which hath ten talents. For unto every one that hath
> shall be given, and he shall have abundance: but from
> him that hath not shall be taken away even that which
> he hath. And cast ye the unprofitable servant into outer
> darkness: there shall be weeping and gnashing of teeth.
> (Matthew 25:28–30)

THE VISION OF THE GOOD
AND FAITHFUL SERVANT

Then the LORD answered me and said: "Write the vision and make it plain on tablets, that he may run who reads it."

—Habakkuk 2:2 NKJV

_____
_____
_____
_____
_____
_____
_____
_____
_____
_____
_____
_____
_____
_____
_____
_____
_____
_____
_____
_____
_____

CHAPTER 18

A VISION WITH ENDURANCE

Cast not away therefore your confidence, which hath great recompence of reward. For ye have need of patience, that, after ye have done the will of God, ye might receive the promise. For yet a little while, and he that shall come will come, and will not tarry.

—Hebrews 10:35–37

He Who promised is faithful. My beloved, I want to tell you with all sincerity of heart that "Jesus Christ is the answer to everything." Before Jesus, my life had no sense of direction, and I was living for nothing. Now I'm traveling kingdom bound! I'm heading somewhere so amazing that it'll take me a whole lifetime to get there. My life has a purpose, and "I'm living for Christ!" He gives me seed, and I get to have the honor of feeding His flock. God's Spirit is moving in my life while I'm locked up in prison only because of His mercy and grace.

My Heavenly Father didn't allow me to die a senseless death in the streets of East Los Angeles (Boyle Heights), where I was raised. He had a plan for me, one that I could not see, nor could anyone else around me—not my teachers, not the cops who would arrest me, not my local community, not even my own family believed in me. And I don't blame anyone because I wasn't heading anywhere but to the grave or a life sentence in prison. The only one who believed in me was God. Every once in a while, though, I would get this little feeling, as if I just knew in my heart that I was destined for more. I would look around and say to myself, *What are you doing here?* But I was stuck there. I didn't know anything else until Jesus set me free! If He can work for me from in here, He can surely work for you out there.

Whatever condition you find yourself in, God can pull you out of it. Look around. God can change it all for you. One day, I will no longer be looking at these prison walls. I will be looking out the window of a skyscraper at a great expanse. The reason we inwardly yearn for more is that He created us for more! The Word opens our eyes, and it gives us a vision of who we can become based on what the Word says He has already done. Everything that we need, He has already made provision for, as His divine power hath given unto us all things that pertain unto life and godliness (2 Peter 1:3).

Also, I don't know if you have given it any thought, but believing is free. It doesn't cost you a dime. All of us, by choice, are going to believe in someone or something, especially during times of trial and testing. Nobody is exempt. "For he maketh his sun to rise on the evil and on the good, and sendeth rain on the just and on the unjust" (Matthew 5:45).

When the floods arise and their streams beat vehemently upon our house, we want to be founded on a rock (Luke 6:48), the Rock—Christ Jesus. That is why we must predetermine that no matter what comes our way, we are not going to be moved or shaken from the truth that we have chosen to stand on.

God has always had our best interests in mind. "And we know that all things work together for good to them that love God, to them who are the called according to his purpose" (Romans 8:28). God knows you better than you may think, and His plans for you are good ones.

> Before I formed thee in the belly I knew thee; and be-
> fore thou earnest forth out of the womb I sanctified
> thee, and I ordained thee a prophet unto the nations.
> (Jeremiah 1:5)

154

> For I know the thoughts that I think toward you, says
> the LORD, thoughts of peace and not of evil, to give
> you a future and a hope. (Jeremiah 29:11 NKJV)

We declare that even in the midst of tribulation, we are going to continue keeping our focus on the only One Who can pull us through it all. We shall keep believing in the God Who created all things and can do all signs and wonders. "For the Lord GOD will help me; therefore shall I not be confounded: therefore have I set my face like a flint, and I know that I shall not be ashamed" (Isaiah 50:7).

When Jesus faced the cross, He kept His face set on the Father. Let us look unto Him!

> Ah Lord GOD! behold, thou hast made the heaven and
> the earth by thy great power and stretched out arm, and
> there is nothing too hard for thee. (Jeremiah 32:17)

And again, our Heavenly Father exclaims through His prophet:

> Behold, I am the LORD, the God of all flesh: is there
> any thing too hard for me? (Jeremiah 32:27)

Let's hear the testimony of one of our forefathers of faith who knew firsthand what it meant to suffer. A testimony that God fashioned and looked ahead through the corridors of time; He preordained for us to be encouraged by it at this very moment.

His name is Job. What can Job tell us?

> Then Job answered the LORD, and said, I know that
> thou canst do every thing, and that no thought can be
> withholden from thee. (Job 42:1–2)

Job happened to be the "Bill Gates" of his time. He then lost it all, and after he went through hell and back, our good God exalted and restored to him double for all his trouble. "Also the LORD gave Job twice as much as he had before" (Job 42:10).

> So the LORD blessed the latter end of Job more than
> his beginning: for he had fourteen thousand sheep, and
> six thousand camels, and a thousand yoke of oxen, and
> a thousand she asses. He had also seven sons and three
> daughters. (Job 42:12–13)

Job did not draw back, and therefore, God's soul had pleasure in Him because he held on in faith (Hebrews 10:38). Job had lost everything—everything except his God, and if you have Him, then that's all you need.

Job bore witness and testified straight out of the page to us:

> I have heard of thee by the hearing of the ear: but now
> mine eye seeth thee. (Job 42:5)

Imagine if Job had quit. He would've missed out on a closer and more personal relationship with God, and he would've forfeited all of his blessings.

What was going through Job's mind and heart? Scripture records him saying, "Though he slay me, yet will I trust in him" (Job 13:15). His face was set like a flint!

Come what may, I'm going to ride it out with God. There's too much Word in my heart, and my eyes have seen His mighty hand move too many times. I'm believing in the living God! The Holy Bible says that there is only one God and only One way to Him, and this is how and what I believe.

> For there is one God, and one mediator between God
> and men, the man Christ Jesus. (1 Timothy 2:5)

Job also believed in this way. For God had made known to him the way and the work of salvation through His only begotten Son.

> For I know that my redeemer liveth, and that he shall
> stand at the latter day upon the earth: and though after
> my skin worms destroy this body, yet in my flesh shall
> I see God: whom I shall see for myself, and mine eyes
> shall behold, and not another; though my reins be con-
> sumed within me. (Job 19:25–27)

Job said, "For I know that my redeemer liveth." He knew that he served a living God and that after he died, one day, he would be resurrected, and in his new flesh, he would see Him. He would see the Messiah standing here on earth with his own eyes. His heart yearned because he knew that God had more for him in the here and now and in the time to come—the afterlife.

When I was sentenced to thirty-seven years, Jesus gave me "the peace of God, which passeth all understanding" (Philippians 4:7). Why? Because my mind stayed on Him. I held on to Scripture with my dear life. The following verses gave me so much hope. Through them, He was telling me that everything was going to be okay and that He was going to change the situation. He was telling me not to let go. Maybe He is telling you the same thing right now.

This was the scripture:

> I would have lost heart, unless I had believed that I
> would see the goodness of the LORD in the land of the
> living. Wait on the LORD; be of good courage, and He
> shall strengthen your heart; wait, I say, on the LORD!
> (Psalm 27:13–14 NKJV)

157

I can't help it. The Holy Bible compels my heart to believe big. It stretches my vision and catapults my imagination, my faith, and my talk into supernatural altitudes!

God will give you the same hope too. Wait on the Lord.

> Now the God of hope fill you with all joy and peace
> in believing, that ye may abound in hope, through the
> power of the Holy Ghost. (Romans 15:13)

Think about it. Job's family was all gone! His businesses were all gone! His properties were all gone! His significant other, her support, was all gone! His God—his God—was still there. He never left!

We read his story, and we say, "Job? Oh yeah, God gave him back double." We can see it because we have the whole story. Job is the one who actually dragged himself from page to page, from chapter to chapter, with a body full of boils as the bark was stripped off him down to the bone. Yet he still worshiped God (Job 1:20). He still retained his integrity (Job 2:9). And "in all this Job did not sin with his lips" (Job 2:10).

Job didn't know how all of that tragedy and adversity was going to end, yet despite all the difficulties and setbacks, he continued without halting! That is why his perseverance is commended.

> My brethren, take the prophets, who spoke in the name
> of the Lord, as an example of suffering and patience.
> Indeed we count them blessed who endure. You have
> heard of the perseverance of Job and seen the end in-
> tended by the Lord—that the Lord is very compassion-
> ate and merciful. (James 5:10–11 NKJV)

Our Heavenly Father had an end intended for Job, as we just read in the scripture. We could see that it was a good end. Well, in the same way, He has an end intended for us, and it's a good one as well. There's a purpose for the storm that we may soon be entering, the one that we are in, or the one that we might be coming out of. Jesus is our boat and the captain of our salvation. He will surely get us to the other side. We've been told, "Weeping may endure for a night, but joy cometh in the morning" (Psalm 30:5).

If anyone knows about our sorrows, it's God, and that's why He has given us His Word so that we may receive comfort and understanding. Let's take heed of the following: It may not be exactly what we want to hear; nevertheless, it's the truth.

> Now no chastening for the present seemeth to be joyous, but grievous: nevertheless afterward it yieldeth the peaceable fruit of righteousness unto them which are exercised thereby. (Hebrews 12:11)

The psalmist sang, "It is good for me that I have been afflicted; that I might learn thy statutes" (Psalm 119:71). Isn't that the truth—that it's during those moments of trial and testing that we learn the Word and have our life-transforming encounters with God? When the fruit is in our hands, when the baby is in our arms, and when we behold the miracle, we can say, "It was all worth it." Take Joseph, for example. He was done wrong by his own brothers and sold into slavery, and when the tables finally turned and he was reigning second-in-command in the Egyptian empire, he didn't take revenge on them. He wasn't bitter or hateful; he was compassionate, merciful, and loving. He responded to them,

> And Joseph said unto them, Fear not: for am I in the place of God? But as for you, ye thought evil against me; but God meant it unto good, to bring to pass, as it is this day, to save much people alive. (Genesis 50:19–20)

Yesterday, after chapel service, I was sharing with some of the Christian brothers that the last time I went down to court for resentencing and got denied, I went through it real bad. But now, I'm glad that I

159

didn't get released because (and I said it with so much joy and enthusiasm that I was leaping!) look, now I'm writing a book, which God is going to use to save souls all over the world!

This is only a season that we are going through; it's not permanent. And before you know it, He is going to change the whole scenery. He can do it before you finish reading this book; it can be before this chapter ends, before this sentence ends, or even before the ending of the next word. I don't know when He'll do it, nor do I know how, but what I can tell you is that "God has an end intended for you. So keep going!" Don't forfeit your blessings, your "vision," or your calling. Keep PUSHing! God knows that you can, I know you can, and that little voice inside you is telling you that you can too!

> There hath no temptation taken you but such as is common to man: but God is faithful, who will not suffer you to be tempted above that ye are able; but will with the temptation also make a way to escape, that ye may be able to bear it. (1 Corinthians 10:13)

Never throw in the towel. God knows how much you can handle, and He will always make a way for you. Grab that towel, gird your waist, and keep on going. Or wrap that towel around your knuckles, make a fist, and go all in for the knockout punch!

YOU. Pow!
ME.　Like that. Again.
YOU. Pow!
ME.　Like that. Again!
YOU. Power! Power! Power!
ME.　See, the enemy messed up. They should've never gotten you started.

My brothers and sisters, the only way that we are going to endure this race and see our vision come to pass is to keep our eyes and faces set and fixed on our Lord and Savior Jesus Christ, always reminding ourselves of everything that He suffered in our place. Bringing into remembrance the following precious and encouraging words: "These things I have spoken unto you, that in me ye might have peace. In the world ye shall have tribulation: but be of good cheer; I have overcome the world" (John 16:33). If we lose sight of Him and His Word, we'll lose our way.

The Holy Bible says,

> Wherefore seeing we also are compassed about with so great a cloud of witnesses, let us lay aside every weight, and the sin which doth so easily beset us, and let us run with patience [endurance] the race that is set before us, looking unto Jesus the author and finisher of our faith; who for the joy that was set before him endured the cross, despising the shame, and is set down at the right hand of the throne of God. For consider him that endured such contradiction of sinners against himself, lest ye be wearied and faint in your minds. Ye have not yet resisted unto blood, striving against sin. (Hebrews 12:1–4)

We have to get rid of the dead weight, and those things that continue to trip us up have to go! We have been through too much and have come too far. Nothing is going to get in our way! We also have to know that there are certain things that we are going to have to go through.

The apostle Paul told his spiritual son, Timothy, "Thou therefore endure hardness, as a good soldier of Jesus Christ" (2 Timothy 2:3). They say that "you have to go through it to get to it." For all my "Jesus soldiers," who are going through it and are determined to get to it, "I salute you!"

God sees you, the heavens see you, and the generations to come will be looking up to you. Keep pushing, pulling, and persevering!

> For God is not unrighteous to forget your work and labour of love, which ye have shewed toward his name, in that ye have ministered to the saints, and do minister. And we desire that every one of you do shew the same diligence to the full assurance of hope unto the end: that ye be not slothful, but followers of them who through faith and patience inherit the promises. (Hebrews 6:10–12)

There's a song that goes, "I have decided to follow Jesus…I have decided to follow Jesus…I have decided to follow Jesus, there's no turning back, no turning back…The world behind me, the cross before me… The world behind me, the cross before me."

As long as my face is set like a flint toward Jesus, I know that I will endure. "Though none go with me, I still will follow…Though none go with me, I still will follow!" Amen.

A VISION WITH ENDURANCE

Then the LORD answered me and said: "Write the vision and make it plain on tablets, that he may run who reads it."

—Habakkuk 2:2 NKJV

_____
_____
_____
_____
_____
_____
_____
_____
_____
_____
_____
_____
_____
_____
_____
_____
_____
_____
_____
_____
_____
_____
_____

A VISION OF THE BEREANS

YOU. Brother Jesse, I want to have faith like yours.

ME.   No, you will believe greater, much greater.

And when the child of God believes more, through that individual, God will do more. Jesus said, "According to your faith be it unto you" (Matthew 9:29).

What you are really asking is that you desire to grow in the spiritual things of God. When I first came to Christ, I desired knowledge, wisdom, and understanding. Day and night, I was in the Word, and everything that the Word said to do, I would do. Why? Because I wanted results. It was all about application and exercising my spiritual muscles. Then one day, I was led to this scripture, and just as simple as that, it worked. Let us never wander away "from the simplicity that is in Christ" (2 Corinthians 11:3). Look how simple it is. It reads,

> If any of you lack wisdom, let him ask of God, that giveth to all men liberally, and upbraideth not; and it shall be given him. (James 1:5)

Maybe nobody else noticed it, but I knew that I knew that He had given it to me! Seeking after God for the sole purpose of getting to know

Him and searching for Him with all your heart with the love and inno-cence of a child is one of the most beautiful experiences of being alive and being a Christian. And one day, you will realize that everything that you ever wanted was already preloaded in your new heart through the incorruptible seed! It doesn't have to stop at wisdom. You can ask Him for anything.

Hear me. The day is coming when God is going to pour out His Spirit again for the second time, which means that the Holy Spirit is going to cause revival to break forth and sweep across the four corners of the earth. He is waving the banner, blowing the trumpet, and sounding the alarm, saying to us, "Gather! Prepare! And assemble yourselves!" My people, shake off that slumber, and dig ditches! Dig ditches! Be-cause the water is coming! (2 Kings 3:16–17).

Don't believe what I say; believe what the Word says, and make sure to cross-examine everything in these pages with the Scripture of God. Do your own research. Jesus's soldiers should be like the "Bereans."

> Then the brethren immediately sent Paul and Silas away by night to Berea. When they arrived, they went into the synagogue of the Jews. These were more fair-minded than those in Thessalonica, in that they received the word with all readiness, and searched the Scriptures daily to find out whether these things were so. (Acts 17:10–11 NKJV)

Like the prophet Ezekiel, when he was in the valley and prophesied to the dry bones and then prophesied to the breath (Ezekiel 37:1–14). So I, too, prophesy to everyone within the reach of these words that "by the will of our Heavenly Father, in the name of Jesus, and through the pow-er of the Holy Spirit, I call forth a generation of Bereans to arise! Arise from your spiritual slumber. I call forth an army of men and women, both young and old, of all ethnicities and from all walks of life, who will fall in love with the Word of God and shall seek the truth by searching the Scriptures, as a deer panteth after the water brooks, amen."

Child of God, if you get ahold of His Word, His Word will take ahold of you. And with His mighty hand, He will transform you. First, we have to ingest it, then consume it. It's so good.

> How sweet are thy words unto my taste! yea, sweeter
> than honey to my mouth! (Psalm 119:103)

That which we put in will eventually come back out. You'll then start speaking His Word, for Jesus said,

> But whosoever drinketh of the water that I shall give
> him shall never thirst; but the water that I shall give him
> shall be in him a well of water springing up into ever-
> lasting life. (John 4:14)

In the same way that the Holy Bible motivates one to believe big, it also motivates one to speak big. Even if at times you don't want to speak, you'll still speak. The prophet Jeremiah once tried to keep silent, but he couldn't.

Let's see his experience.

> Then I said, I will not make mention of him, nor speak
> any more in his name. But his word was in mine heart
> as a burning fire shut up in my bones, and I was weary
> with forbearing, and I could not stay. (Jeremiah 20:9)

He said that he was weary of holding it back until he could no longer! And this is a good thing because, when we begin speaking His Word, that's where the molding, changing, and transforming take place—not only in us but also in the domain around us. When we speak His Word, He begins operating, and He extends His mighty arm.

> O house of Israel, cannot I do with you as this potter? saith the LORD. Behold, as the clay is in the potter's hand, so are ye in mine hand, O house of Israel. (Jeremiah 18:6)

One of the things that the Word changes is our thinking. When we change the way we think, we will change the way we act. When our mind changes, which is internal, our whole external outlook on life is revolutionized. Perspective is everything. Ephesians 4:23 says, "And be renewed in the spirit of your mind," and, "Be ye transformed by the renewing of your mind" (Romans 12:2) by the reading of the Word.

Our vocabulary will actually begin to change as well. We then stop talking about doubt, fear, and defeat over ourselves and others. Our words become filled with faith, courage, and life—with hope!

As children of God, who were created in His image and after His likeness and who were given dominion (Genesis 1:26), we begin to talk like Him. How does He talk? Our God "calleth those things which be not as though they were" (Romans 4:17).

Please read with me the following scripture:

> We having the same spirit of faith, according as it is written, I believed, and therefore have I spoken; we also believe, and therefore speak. (2 Corinthians 4:13)

When we, as believers, speak what is written, we can bank on it. Why or how? Because it's His Word that we are speaking. God says in His Word, "I create the fruit of the lips" (Isaiah 57:19). He fashions and eventually gives our words physical form.

God spoke His Word, and the prophet and the scribe wrote it down and made a record. Once it's captured on the page, it remains there alive, in seed form. Then you come around, read it, receive it in faith, and meditate on it, and you loose it out of your mouth, and God takes over!

The prophet Isaiah speaks about this function.

> For as the rain cometh down, and the snow from heaven, and returneth not thither, but watereth the earth, and maketh it bring forth and bud, that it may give seed to the sower, and bread to the eater: so shall my word be that goeth forth out of my mouth: it shall not return unto me void, but it shall accomplish that which I please, and it shall prosper in the thing whereto I sent it. (Isaiah 55:10–11)

God's Word produces, and it never returns to Him empty. It has already left His mouth; it now needs to leave yours. What does His Word accomplish? What does His Word produce? Well, that all depends on what scriptures we have spoken. Was it healing, power, a blessing, or peace? We have a whole Book full of seeds to speak to and to plant from. His Word never returns to Him empty or void, nor can it ever run out.

A Berean is aware of this and uses it to his advantage. For the Bereans of today are like an elite group of "special forces" of highly trained men and women in searching and applying the Scriptures. They are also very fruitful because they are full of seeds, which means the more they consume, the more seeds they can plant in their hearts and speak to others. Everywhere they go, they go forth, scattering seed. Their vision is just not talk. No, not at all. They are laboring for it.

You see, the Bereans have taken heed to where it is written,

> In the morning sow thy seed, and in the evening withold not thine hand: for thou knowest not whether shall prosper, either this or that, or whether they both shall be alike good. (Ecclesiastes 11:6)

When it was Joshua's turn to go from assistant to leader, God told him the way to success. He said to him, as He says to us,

> Only be thou strong and very courageous, that thou mayest observe to do according to all the law, which Moses my servant commanded thee: turn not from it to the right hand or to the left, that thou mayest prosper withersoever thou goest.This book of the law shall not depart out of thy mouth; but thou shalt meditate therein day and night, that thou mayest observe to do according to all that is written therein: for then thou shalt make thy way prosperous, and then thou shalt have good success. (Joshua 1:7–8)

We are to meditate in His Word day and night without turning from it to the right hand or the left so that no matter what's happening around us, we will be prosperous and have good success. Day and night, seed-time and harvest, seedtime and in-between time, we are to be reading and speaking. A child of God can sow so much that it can get to a point where it's harvest time all the time, all year round, every day, and in all areas of life; it's a constant reaping! Growth's springing up everywhere.

Being always in the Word is an exercise. That's why the Bereans train up in the Word, and they exert themselves in it. The more they get into the things of the Spirit, the more they perform supernaturally in the physical. These are the ones who do the things that the Word says they can do. Their function and performance are in direct proportion to their prophecy. And their prophecy is in direct proportion to their faith, and as you already know, "so then faith cometh by hearing, and hearing by the word of God" (Romans 10:17). How can you hear the Word all the time? Easy, press the repeat button, the one that says "MEDITATE" on it. Use what you have and build it up.

> Having then gifts differing according to the grace that is given to us, whether prophecy, let us prophesy according to the proportion of faith. (Romans 12:6)

Little Word eaten, little Word spoken. If you want to prophesy big and if you want God to do big things, then you know what you need to do. Get in that Word—Berean style!

The fulfillment of your vision is also in direct proportion to your relationship with the Word of God. Remember Joseph's dream? That was a pretty big vision, and he went through a lot to get to it, but he held on to it, and the LORD Almighty brought it to pass.

Scripture says,

> Moreover he called for a famine upon the land: he brake the whole staff of bread. He sent a man before them, even Joseph, who was sold for a servant: whose feet they hurt with fetters: he was laid in iron: until the time that his word came: **the word of the LORD tried him**. The king sent and loosed him; even the ruler of the people, and let him go free. He made him lord of his house, and ruler of all his substance: to bind his princes at his pleasure; and teach his senators wisdom. (Psalms 105:16–22, emphasis added)

Look at how much revolved around Joseph's vision! Obviously, the vision was bigger than Joseph. The scripture says that until Joseph's word (his dream, his vision) came to pass, the Word of the LORD tried him, tested him, and refined him. Like a goldsmith beating on his metals, the Word fused him, purged him, and shaped him into a new man—into the leader who could carry out such a vision. Big vision, big mission!

Through it all, Joseph stayed in the things of God. The Holy Bible says, "And the LORD was with Joseph" (Genesis 39:2).

YOU. I believe! I believe! I believe! Praise God! I believe!

ME.   Wonderful! All glory to God! Now apply what you believe.

YOU. Let's keep going. What else?

ME.   Yes, we just need to summarize real quick what we've studied thus far.

YOU. No, no, I get it. You are right. To be like Jesus (Christlike), I'm going to need a real big vision.

ME.   Congratulations! You see it. However, I still want you to have a firm understanding of the *hows* and the *whys*.

We are also going to learn the dynamics and mechanics of three prophecies: the one made by Jesus, the one spoken by Joel, and the one made by the prophet Isaiah. These are end-time prophecies, and they agree with and enhance the point and the message that is going to be presented here. "The latter rain of the Holy Spirit."

So when Satan comes and tries to steal your confidence or confuse you, you'll be caught "standing watch" with your faith built upon the Rock.

> When any one heareth the word of the kingdom, and understandeth it not, then cometh the wicked one, and catcheth away that which was sown in his heart. This is he which received seed by the way side. (Matthew 13:19)

In Jesus's name, this seed will not fall anywhere but on a good and fertile heart, and we are looking to receive a produce, an increase, and a blessing of a thousand times over, as the scripture says in Deuteronomy 1:11. So be it unto you! (Amen.)

Remember, my brothers and sisters, that all Bereans are Christians, but not all Christians are like the Bereans.

Question: Are you a Berean?

A VISION OF THE BEREANS

Then the LORD answered me and said: "Write the vision and make it plain on tablets, that he may run who reads it."

—Habakkuk 2:2 NKJV

_____
_____
_____
_____
_____
_____
_____
_____
_____
_____
_____
_____
_____
_____
_____
_____
_____
_____
_____
_____
_____
_____
_____
_____

CHAPTER 20

A VISION FILLED WITH THE LATTER RAIN

Bereans! Pull up your bootstraps and let's go! Have "your feet shod with the preparation of the gospel of peace" (Ephesians 6:15). Yes, preparation can only come through practice, and we will only perform to the degree that we practice. Today, we are preparing and training for the major leagues and the championships of tomorrow.

One can tell when a person is going somewhere in life by how much heart they put into their craft, their sport, or their career. Since the child of God has already attained everlasting life through Christ Jesus, everything on earth can be put on the line. We're all in! We have nothing to lose. With that in mind, we are going to embark upon scripture systematically.

> For precept must be upon precept, precept upon pre-
> cept; line upon line, line upon line; here a little, and
> there a little. (Isaiah 28:10)

Nugget by nugget, jewel by jewel, we make progress and advance in the knowledge and wisdom of God.

QUICK SUMMARY

Jesus, prior to going away (ascending to heaven), says, "The works that I do shall he do also; and greater works than these shall he do" (John 14:12). Jesus would be able to do the greater works through us because the Holy Spirit would come and dwell in our hearts. This was granted by our Heavenly Father.

He is the One:

> Who also has sealed us and given us the Spirit in our hearts as a guarantee. (2 Corinthians 1:22 NKJV)

For Jesus to do "whatever" or "anything," we will first have to ask. Also, the Spirit that gives power will be poured out on all flesh on the day of Pentecost, which will take place not many days from that night. When Christ resurrected, He said to the apostles, "For John truly baptized with water; but ye shall be baptized with the Holy Ghost not many days hence" (Acts 1:5). The Spirit being poured out on all flesh was a prophecy that had been spoken of in the Old Testament by the prophet Joel.

After the Spirit was to be poured out, the prophecy given by Jesus pertaining to "works and the greater works" would be fulfilled, but only in part. Why only in part? It's because this prophecy encompasses the whole period of "the latter days," as does the prophecy of Joel, which is also substantiated by the prophet Isaiah. For as long as the Holy Spirit is here on earth, inside the believers, His power through the hands and mouths of His children will be made manifest and will abound through miracles. However, the greatest move of the Holy Spirit is yet to be seen!

Let's continue here. You see, nobody discounts the fact that when a believer gets saved, he or she receives the indwelling of the Holy Spirit. So why would anyone discount the by-product, which is the signs, works, and wonders?

Jesus said that "signs shall follow them that believe" (Mark 16:17). "Signs will follow" means that they are secondary. The rationale is basic: First, you get the milk, and then you can make the cheese, but you can't make the cheese without the milk. It's the same thing; one cannot produce miracles without the Spirit of God.

> And they went forth, and preached every where, the
> Lord working with them, and confirming the word with
> signs following. Amen. (Mark 16:20)

They went out preaching, speaking, and petitioning. And God was not only with them but also in them! Jesus was not only working with them but also through them—through the Holy Spirit. He was confirming the Word spoken through miracles. As long as the Holy Spirit is present, miracles will present themselves. The Son will do, confirm, and perform!

To fully grasp and understand what was about to take place, we need to know what the prophet Joel spoke in his prophecy.

Remember, my young Bereans, that the Holy Bible interprets itself. Scripture interprets scripture.

Let's unpack it here in the book of Acts.

> But this is that which was spoken by the prophet Joel;
> And it shall come to pass in the last days, saith God, I
> will pour out of my Spirit upon all flesh: and your sons
> and your daughters shall prophesy, and your young men
> shall see visions, and your old men shall dream dreams.
> (Acts 2:16–17)

Though the prophet Joel initially made mention of this prophecy in the Old Testament (Joel 2:28–32), it was God Who was speaking through the prophet. In the same way, Peter is now standing and, with a raised voice, is speaking under the inspiration of the same Spirit of God.

And under that unction, Peter gives us some clarity and insight of great value—concerning this event—of "the outpouring of the Holy Spirit."

Prophecy is spoken by man, but it comes directly from God. It is not man's word to man; it's God's Word to mankind. Scripture says this in regard to prophecy:

> Knowing this first, that no prophecy of the scripture is of any private interpretation. For the prophecy came not in old time by the will of man: but holy men of God spake as they were moved by the Holy Ghost. (2 Peter 1:20–21)

Prophecy is never subject to any private interpretation. Since the origin of the prophecy is from God, the interpretation and explanation belong to Him. In other words, we can't make a prophecy mean what we want it to mean. The Scriptures and the Holy Spirit tell us what a prophecy means and when it's being fulfilled or has been fulfilled.

The Holy Bible says, "For the testimony of Jesus is the spirit of prophecy" (Revelation 19:10). Peter is under this prophetic inspiration, and one of the first things that jump out of the scripture and call our attention is that he uses the term "in the last days."

> And it shall come to pass in the **last days**. (Acts 2:17, Emphasis added)

We will now compare it to what the prophet Joel said:

> And it shall come to pass **afterward**. (Joel 2:28, Emphasis added)

Joel used the word *afterward*, which simply points to the future, specifically "the last days." "The last days" is also synonymous with the term *end-time*. Another expression that is used in the scripture to refer to the last days is "latter days" or "latter times."

Here's how "latter days" is used in the book of Daniel:

> Now I am come to make thee understand what shall befall thy people in the **latter days**: for yet the vision is for many days. (Daniel 10:14, emphasis added)

Here, the apostle Paul encourages his spiritual son, Timothy, saying,

> Now the Spirit speaketh expressly, that in the **latter times** some shall depart from the faith, giving heed to seducing spirits, and doctrines of devils. (1 Timothy 4:1, emphasis added)

The word *latter* is used to refer to "the last," "the future," or the "last of all." The word *latter* is also used to signal out "the second of two things"—the *latter* growth, the *latter* crop, "the *latter* rain!" It's the second round. This word, *latter*, will help us unlock this message and wrap it back up again.

We are back in the book of Acts and still in the same verse, but we are going to put it under the microscope.

> I will pour out of my Spirit upon all flesh. (Acts 2:17)

Joel's version says the same thing, with only one little difference. Let's see if you can catch it.

> I will pour out my spirit upon all flesh. (Joel 2:28)

Do you see it? It is the word *of*. The book of Acts says, "I will pour out 'of ' my Spirit," while the book of Joel just says, "I will pour out my spirit upon all flesh." So you may be saying, "Why is this important, or what difference does it make?" Well, it makes a big difference that's enough to blow the scales off our eyes when we learn what God is conveying to us here through the scriptures for this time and generation.

In the next verse, Peter repeats the same line:

> And on my servants and on my handmaidens I will pour out in those days of my Spirit; and they shall prophesy. (Acts 2:18)

Peter mentions the same thing twice, pertaining to the pouring out of His Spirit. This pouring out or "outpouring" is figurative for water or rain. Let's back this up with the Word.

> For I will pour water upon him that is thirsty, and floods upon the dry ground: I will pour my spirit upon thy seed, and my blessing upon thine offspring. (Isaiah 44:3)

> Until the spirit be poured upon us from on high, and the wilderness be a fruitful field, and the fruitful field be counted for a forest. (Isaiah 32:15)

> Rain down, you heavens, from above, and let the skies pour down righteousness; let the earth open, let them bring forth salvation, and let righteousness spring up together. I, the LORD, have created it. (Isaiah 45:8 NKJV)

We finished reading three scriptures, of which the first two spoke of the pouring of the Spirit as a reference to water. However, the "latter" verse, the third one, was a bit different. It spoke about the "heavens raining down righteousness" and the "earth opening and them bringing forth salvation."

Evidently, we know Who is the One Who rained down righteousness from above and the only One Who can bring forth salvation on earth. His name is Jesus, and He does it through the Holy Spirit. The Holy Spirit works through man, for the scripture says, "Let them bring forth salvation!"

Since we have entered into the subject of rain, we might as well glean a slight knowledge of the rain patterns of that place and time, along with picking up a few kernels of insight into their agriculture.

Rain, for the children of Israel, was very important, and a lot of their lives and culture revolved around it. The most important thing for them was to love and worship God. Remember, when a lawyer tested Jesus, asking Him, "Master, which is the great commandment in the law?" (Matthew 22:36). What was our Master's response?

> Jesus said unto him, Thou shalt love the Lord thy God
> with all thy heart, and with all thy soul, and with all thy
> mind. (Matthew 22:37)

Rain is perhaps the second-most important thing, if not close to it. If it doesn't rain for long time, famine will sweep across the land. Water is life, and without rain, life cannot be sustained.

God is also the One Who was and is in control of the rain. Many times, and throughout many droughts, men and women have prayed for rain. The Holy Bible makes a record of when the prophet Elijah prayed earnestly and fervently for rain. It also states that he was a man with a nature like ours, meaning that he was not perfect, and if he can do it, then so can we because, at the end of the day, it's His power that does the miracle.

> Elias was a man subject to like passions as we are, and he prayed earnestly that it might not rain: and it rained not on the earth by the space of three years and six months. And he prayed again, and the heaven gave rain, and the earth brought forth her fruit. (James 5:17–18)

Man can pray for rain, but only God can send it.

The Palestine region was very dry and extremely arid, and every drop of rain counted. As did the timing of when the rain came. It was crucial that it arrive at its proper time, in its due season.

When rain is mentioned here, we are talking about two periods, times, and seasons. This knowledge and perspective will definitely help us grasp the meaning of the prophecy of Joel and how it applies to us, the church, and all of Israel.

When Joel spoke about God pouring out His Spirit, he said,

> And it shall come to pass afterward, that I will pour out my spirit upon all flesh; and your sons and your daughters shall prophesy, your old men shall dream dreams, your young men shall see visions: and also upon the servants and upon the handmaids in those days will I pour out my spirit. (Joel 2:28–29)

Joel mentioned God pouring out His Spirit twice. We will also take notice that a few verses prior to these two, he speaks about two rainy seasons. This was spoken during a time of great famine, in which the land had been decimated by the lack of rain.

The prophet said,

> Be glad then, ye children of Zion, and rejoice in the LORD your God: for he hath given you the former rain moderately, and he will cause to come down for you the rain, the former rain, and the latter rain in the first

month. And the floors shall be full of wheat, and the fats
shall overflow with wine and oil. (Joel 2:23–24)

A crop would need both rains in order to produce one harvest. It
needed the former rain and the latter rain.

As true and valuable as this knowledge of the "times and seasons"
was to the farmer, so likewise does it apply to the Christian of today,
who is also waiting.

Scripture encourages us by saying,

Therefore be patient, brethren, until the coming of the
Lord. See how the farmer waits for the precious fruit
of the earth, waiting patiently for it until it receives the
early and latter rain. (James 5:7 NKJV)

Though it's two separate and different rain seasons, they complete
one cycle, and they both, working together, lead to one goal: "The Harvest." God has set these laws in order, as we are told in the following
verse:

Then I will give you the rain for your land in its season,
the early rain and the latter rain, that you may gather in
your grain, your new wine, and your oil. (Deuteronomy
11:14 NKJV)

All the praying, the different seasons, all the working, toiling the
land, the patience, being hopeful—all so that the precious fruit of the
land may be gathered in. The harvest, a time of great joy!

THE FIRST SHOWERS

The former rain took place in the winter. It was the first rain, which
would soften the soil and cause the germination of the seed that was

sown. These first showers encouraged growth, causing the tender shoots to spring up. "First the blade, then the ear, after that the full corn in the ear" (Mark 4:28).

THE SECOND SHOWERS

The latter rain showers took place in the spring. They caused the crops to receive the final push that they needed, quickening the grain to swell, ripen, and come to full maturity. After this final stage, comes the sickle. "But when the fruit is brought forth, immediately he putteth in the sickle, because the harvest is come" (Mark 4:29).

The children of Israel were an agricultural society, and though they knew how to work the soil, their lifestyle demanded that they exercise a lot of faith. There are a lot of detriments when it comes to farming. The last thing that a farmer needed was a swarm of locusts, fires, or drought, and that's just to name a few examples. No, the farmer "had his face set like a flint." He was all in, and in his heart, all would end up alright. So how did they use their faith? Or what is faith?

> Now faith is the substance of things hoped for, the evidence of things not seen. (Hebrews 11:1)

Even before planting, the sower, through his vision, can see the fields, orchards, and acres overflowing with the best fruit that the earth can produce. That's his vision; it's what he hopes for. He hopes that it will happen and that it will come to pass. This is a spiritual hope that is practiced with the physical senses. It is a lively hope (1 Peter 1:3), and it motivates!

> Now hope does not disappoint, because the love of God
> has been poured out in our hearts by the Holy Spirit
> who was given to us. (Romans 5:5 NKJV)

Hope does not disappoint because the love of God has been poured out in our hearts by the Holy Spirit—by God! Hope does not disappoint because "love never fails" (1 Corinthians 13:8 NKJV). We now have three things working together for good: "And now abide faith, hope, love, these three; but the greatest of these is love" (1 Corinthians 13:13 NKJV). This is a beautiful and powerful combination here. We have a love that doesn't fail, and we are left with faith and hope. Again, "now faith is the substance of things hoped for, the evidence of things not seen."

Now the reason why hope does not disappoint is because hope pushes and activates the faith—faith that God will do it, and thus, it is considered received and done!

Jesus is my faith! You see, the farmer can already see it in his hand through the eyes of his heart. Now is there something that you can already see that hasn't happened yet? What are you hoping for or expecting in faith that Jesus, in due season, will give you? Is our assurance in scriptures like 2 Corinthians 1:20?

> For all the promises of God in him are yea, and in him
> Amen, unto the glory of God by us.

What I am about to show you will revolutionize your whole life if you learn how it works and apply it. ("Faith is the substance of things hoped for, the evidence of things not seen.") In general, everything is done by faith, and faith in and of itself is unbiased. It doesn't question; it just obeys. The job of faith is "to do," but it has to be directed, and it must be commanded. That's where the substance comes in. Substance is measurable, and it's measured by the "things" that are being "hoped" for. If you hope for little things, then you will have little substance, but if you hope for big things, then you'll have big substance. So, it's "hope" that pushes and activates "faith." Hope places a demand on faith. What, then, is hope? The bottom line is that hope is a CONTAINER that holds

185

your vision or visions. And you can have as many containers as you want or as you can hope for.

Let's make it even more simple. For the believer in Jesus, hope is the container that holds and is filled with your vision. Faith is the vessel that brings it to you. God is the source—the One Who does the giving and the distribution! Without Him, we can do nothing. (Are my shipping containers full, or are they empty?)

The substance, therefore, ends up being the "balance" of the amount of vision that your hope containers carry.

We can't overlook or forget the second part. "The evidence of things not seen." Faith is the evidence of things not seen, "yet!" Why is it the evidence of things? Because if you really believe in something, then there's going to be some evidence that you and others can point a finger at. There are going to be action steps being taken, and following our words, it's not only talking but also doing. The scripture is clear about this: "Thus also faith by itself, if it does not have works, is dead" (James 2:17 NKJV). Your barns should be built and ready way before the harvest comes. What did Jesus say to His disciples? "I go to prepare a place for you" (John 14:2).

The former rain is related to winter, plowing, sowing, and toil. Waiting. Patience. Silence. The seed was in the darkness. It was when the thing planted took root downward.

The latter rain relates to the manifestation of a vision, to the reward, and to the fullness of joy! It's about spring, reaping, and the end. The time of bearing fruit upward and outward!

The end or completion of what? The finishing work, "the harvest of the earth," is the Lord's work of salvation, the salvation and gathering of souls! The calling and the process do not change—to the Jew first and then to the Gentile. As the apostle Paul wrote under the inspiration of the Holy Spirit,

> For I am not ashamed of the gospel of Christ: for it
> is the power of God unto salvation to every one that

believeth; to the Jew first, and also to the Greek. (Romans 1:16)

Salvation is available to everyone who believes. That's why "the everlasting gospel to preach unto them that dwell on the earth, and to every nation, and kindred, and tongue, and people" (Revelation 14:6) needs to be pronounced. Jesus Christ is salvation to the ends of the earth.

We can, therefore, conclude that there's going to be a second rain, the latter rain of the Holy Spirit, which shall be poured out to accomplish the finishing final work of the Lord's harvest.

The first time that the former rain of the Holy Spirit was poured out was on the church on the day of Pentecost. This is when the church was birthed. Scripture says in Acts 2:17,

> And it shall come to pass in the last days, saith God, I will pour out of my Spirit upon all flesh.

During this first outpouring, the phrase, "I will pour out 'of ' my Spirit upon all flesh," tells us that it was only a portion. And we know through the scripture that a second outpouring would follow. This is told to us in the following verse of Acts 2:18:

> And on my servants and on my handmaidens I will pour out in those days of my Spirit.

Let's clarify that the Holy Spirit never left, so it's not like He is coming back down again, for He lives in our hearts. What is going to happen is that there is going to be a move of God through the Holy Spirit like it has never been witnessed on earth before.

> The Lord is not slack concerning his promise, as some men count slackness; but is longsuffering to us-ward,

not willing that any should perish, but that all should come to repentance. (2 Peter 3:9)

The Holy Spirit will be poured out in anticipation of a great harvest—of His harvest. Yes, this is His harvest; it's His planning, planting, watering, increasing, and gathering up. He is the harvester! And we get the privilege and honor of going out into His fields.

Therefore said he unto them, The harvest truly is great, but the labourers are few: pray ye therefore the Lord of the harvest, that he would send forth labourers into his harvest. (Luke 10:2)

This is the time when "they that be wise shall shine as the brightness of the firmament" (Daniel 12:3).

The former rain of the Holy Spirit was poured out on the day of Pentecost, an event that took place approximately two thousand years ago. At that time, their world was limited to the surrounding region. And from Jerusalem, the message through the Spirit began spreading, causing awakening and revival. However, America and other parts of the world had not been discovered yet. The access to those souls wasn't there. So when Jesus said, "Go therefore and make disciples of all the nations, baptizing them in the name of the Father and of the Son and of the Holy Spirit" (Matthew 28:19 NKJV), they only went so far. But it didn't stop with them, because here we are today, STILL PUSHING under the same name, the same Spirit, and the same commission.

So far, we have covered in this section that the former rain of the Holy Spirit has already been poured out. And we are currently waiting for the latter rain to arrive. Now we shall go a little bit deeper into both of these events through the lens of the prophet Isaiah.

> And in that day there shall be a root of Jesse, which shall
> stand for an ensign of the people; to it shall the Gentiles
> seek: and his rest shall be glorious. (Isaiah 11:10)

What is Isaiah saying through this prophecy? This is talking about salvation through Jesus Christ for the Jews (the people) and for the Gentiles (the rest of the nations—the World). However, for the most part, the Jewish people did not accept Jesus as the promised Messiah, the Savior. "For God hath concluded them all in unbelief, that he might have mercy upon all" (Romans 11:32).

Paul sheds a lot of light on this subject.

> For I would not, brethren, that ye should be ignorant of
> this mystery, lest ye should be wise in your own con-
> ceits; that blindness in part is happened to Israel, until
> the fulness of the Gentiles be come in. (Romans 11:25)

The Gentiles began getting saved and receiving the gift of the Holy Spirit in mass numbers after Pentecost. Paul mentions that this was even spoken of by Moses.

> But I say, Did not Israel know? First Moses saith, I will
> provoke you to jealousy by them that are no people, and
> by a foolish nation I will anger you. (Romans 10:19)

Paul also lets us know (without a shadow of a doubt) that the Gentiles becoming partakers of the spiritual things of God is a fulfillment of the prophecy written in Isaiah 11:10. He says,

> And again, Esaias saith, There shall be a root of Jesse,
> and he that shall rise to reign over the Gentiles; in him
> shall the Gentiles trust. (Romans 15:12)

189

The Gentiles are that "foolish nation," which we know to be the "church." Isaiah 11:10 is the first outpouring of the Holy Spirit—the former rain.

The prophet Isaiah also makes mention of the latter rain in the following prophecy:

> And it shall come to pass in that day, that **the Lord shall set his hand again the second time** to recover the remnant of his people, which shall be left, from Assyria, and from Egypt, and from Pathros, and from Cush, and from Elam, and from Shinar, and from Hamath, and from the islands of the sea. And he shall set up an ensign for **the nations**, and shall assemble the outcasts of Israel, and gather together the dispersed of Judah from the four corners of the earth. (Isaiah 11:11–12, emphasis added)

The hand of the LORD is the move of the Holy Spirit in demonstration of His power. So right here, where it says that "the Lord shall set his hand again the second time," we can conclude that it was already set the first time, which was spoken of in the previous verse and confirmed by the apostle Paul's reference to Isaiah 11:10.

What can happen when the hand of God comes upon a man of God?

> But now bring me a minstrel [musician]. And it came to pass, when the minstrel played, that the hand of the LORD came upon him. And he said, Thus saith the LORD, Make this valley full of ditches. (2 Kings 3:15–16)

The prophet Elisha prophesied when the hand of the LORD came upon him! We will now see the experience of the prophet Ezekiel:

> The hand of the LORD was upon me, and carried me
> out in the spirit of the LORD, and set me down in the
> midst of the valley which was full of bones. (Ezekiel
> 37:1)

Did Ezekiel have a vision, or was he actually teleported, like Philip
was, after he baptized the eunuch in the New Testament? And when
Philip was caught away, was it by God's hand, or, I mean, the hand of
the Spirit (same thing)?

> And when they were come up out of the water, the
> Spirit of the Lord caught away Philip, that the eunuch
> saw him no more: and he went on his way rejoicing.
> But Philip was found at Azotus: and passing through
> he preached in all the cities, till he came to Caesarea.
> (Acts 8:39–40)

The second time that He sets His hand, "the latter rain," it will be
to recover Israel from the four corners of the earth. "And he shall set up
an ensign for the nations" (Isaiah 11:11–12). Jesus Christ is that banner!
The word *nations* here in Hebrew means "a foreign nation, a Gentile
nation, a heathen people, non-Jewish." Remember that the apostle Paul
just told us a while ago that "I [He] will provoke you to jealousy by
them that are no people, and by a foolish nation I [He] will anger you"
(Romans 10:19). That nation is the church.

So we see that when He sets His hand again the second time, it'll
be a worldwide move of His Spirit upon Israel and the church! "There
is neither Jew nor Greek, there is neither bond nor free, there is neither
male nor female: for ye are all one in Christ Jesus" (Galatians 3:28).
Glory!

> And so all Israel shall be saved: as it is written,There
> shall come out of Sion the Deliverer, and shall turn

away ungodliness from Jacob: for this is my covenant unto them, when I shall take away their sins. (Romans 11:26–27)

Let's wrap this up. Scripture tells us through its pages that the former rain of the Holy Spirit had already fallen, and it was primarily on the Gentiles. And we are aware through prophetic Scripture that the latter rain will be received by both Jews and Gentiles—Israel and the church.

The purpose of the latter rain is to bring the crops to maturity; the rain causes the grain or the fruit to swell or become filled with sweet juice. This translates into us being filled with the Spirit like never before. What does this mean for the believer? It means the supernatural, the miraculous!

Ye are a living epistle, a living letter! "Known and read of all men" (2 Corinthians 3:2). You are a manifestation of what has been written in your heart by the Holy Spirit, but when this second shower hits you, the vision that has been sown, written, and cultivated in your heart through meditation will be projected onto the canvas of the world stage for the glory of God in the mighty name of Jesus!

Jesus really meant it when He said,

> Ye are the light of the world. A city that is set on an hill cannot be hid. (Matthew 5:14)

> Let your light so shine before men, that they may see your good works, and glorify your Father which is in heaven. (Matthew 5:16)

I prophesy to every believing heart upon the authority of the scripture (John 14:12) that this will be when the sons of the kingdom shall rise up and do the "greater works" that our Lord and Savior Jesus Christ said in His prophecy that we would do! Amen. Our Master tells us, "Heaven and earth shall pass away: but my words shall not pass away"

(Mark 13:31). His every Word shall come to pass, and His every prophecy shall be fulfilled.

My Christian brothers and sisters, I know that through our vision,
we can look far ahead into the future at what can be, and in faith, we
can snatch it and lock on to it. All of that is good; we look forward to
the coming of "the latter rain," and that's good. We look forward to the
coming of the Lord to rule and reign with Him for a thousand years. We
look to the new heaven and the new earth, and all of that is good. Vision
is good. Prophecies are good. Hope is good. And all of these good things
satellite around Jesus, which is commendable. But today, the person of
Jesus Christ is to take precedence in our lives, and everything else shall
fall into place all on its own.

Now is the day of salvation (2 Corinthians 6:2). The day of salvation is today, and souls are in the balance. Everything that we need to
get the job done today, we already have. We have the Holy Spirit, and
we have the Holy Bible; everything else is secondary. Whom God calls,
He equips!

I believe that the following scripture suits the occasion well. Here
is the True Vine speaking forth to every generation:

> Say not ye, There are yet four months, and then cometh
> harvest? behold, I say unto you, Lift up your eyes, and
> look on the fields; for they are white already to harvest.
> (John 4:35)

Let's live with the expectation that Jesus may be coming for us
"today."

> Therefore, my beloved brethren, be ye stedfast, un-
> moveable, always abounding in the work of the Lord,
> forasmuch as ye know that your labour is not in vain in
> the Lord. (1 Corinthians 15:58)

A VISION FILLED WITH THE LATTER RAIN

> Then the LORD answered me and said: "Write the vision and make it plain on tablets, that he may run who reads it."
>
> —Habakkuk 2:2 NKJV

_____

_____

_____

_____

_____

_____

_____

_____

_____

_____

_____

_____

_____

_____

_____

_____

_____

_____

_____

_____

CHAPTER 21

SEEING VISIONS
AND DREAMING DREAMS

Through the Holy Spirit, we can see visions and dream dreams. These are not your average normal dreams, for all men and women dream. Quite the contrary, these are prophetic visions and prophetic dreams in which the child of God is to prophesy and speak forth! And thus, the power of God is released into the air, the atmosphere, and the cosmos! Once we release His Word or His message, He takes over! He said in the Word, "I create the fruit of the lips" (Isaiah 57:19).

If you only knew how God wants to use you as His mouthpiece and broadcast machine down here on earth. The Old Testament echoes with scriptures that read, "Who will I send?" or "I looked and there was no man to send." And I remember as a young Christian saying, "I'm right here, Lord. Send me!"

"He creates the fruit of the lips." The word *create* is the same Hebrew word used in Genesis. Glory! There is power in the name of Jesus! He is still working, moving, and creating.

> In the beginning God **created** the heaven and the earth.
> (Genesis 1:1, emphasis added)

The Holy Bible teaches us that He created the heavens and the earth by what He said. And now He is able to create through your prophecy of His Word. He creates the fruit of your lips, the utterances. He forms, fashions, frames, and furnishes them!

> And God said, Let there be light: and there was light. (Genesis 1:3)

We are to speak His Word to the situation and the circumstance, irrespective of how it looks or feels. That's how God did it. "And the earth was without form, and void; and darkness was upon the face of the deep. And the Spirit of God moved upon the face of the waters" (Genesis 1:2). God did not speak of what He saw, for all that could be seen was darkness and chaos. But the concealed and conceivable potential was there, and the Holy Spirit was also there, just hovering over the face of the waters, ready to give body and form to God's words! Today, we have His Word and His Spirit. Child of God, speak!

> Then the LORD put forth his hand, and touched my mouth. And the LORD said unto me, Behold, I have put my words in thy mouth. See, I have this day set thee over the nations and over the kingdoms, to root out, and to pull down, and to destroy, and to throw down, to build, and to plant. (Jeremiah 1:9–10)

The Holy Spirit inhabits our praises and the prophecy that is made in His name and according to His Word. That is why worshiping Him is so powerful.

> But thou art holy, O thou that inhabitest the praises of Israel. (Psalm 22:3)

But You are holy, enthroned in the praises of Israel. (Psalm 22:3 NKJV)

He inhabits, enthrones, takes a seat, and dwells in the praises, as if taking residence in them. And when has anyone ever praised without the use of the scriptures? We praise Him that He does hearken to His Word.

You will also declare a thing, and it will be established for you; so light will shine on your ways. When they cast you down, and you say, "Exaltation will come!" then He will save the humble person. (Job 22:28–29 NKJV)

"Let us hold fast the confession of our hope without wavering, for He who promised is faithful" (Hebrews 10:23 NKJV). If you received a word from the Lord, a vision, or a dream, hold fast to that confession, and don't be led astray by what your senses may tell you. Make God's promises to you more real than anything else.

For God speaketh once, yea twice, yet man perceiveth it not. In a dream, in a vision of the night, when deep sleep falleth upon men, in slumberings upon the bed; then he openeth the ears of men, and sealeth their instruction. (Job 33:14–16)

It's our job to speak, and it's His to create. And because it's His Word, He'll confirm it, and He will perform it!

That confirmeth the word of his servant, and performeth the counsel of his messengers; that saith to Jerusalem, Thou shalt be inhabited; and to the cities of Judah, Ye shall be built, and I will raise up the decayed places thereof. (Isaiah 44:26)

Can I ask you for something? When His Word comes to you, in whatever way it comes, and it will, can you please write it down? Yes, write it and speak it. Prophesy it!

> And it shall come to pass in the last days, saith God, I will pour out of my Spirit upon all flesh: and your sons and your daughters shall prophesy, and your young men shall see visions, and your old men shall dream dreams. (Acts 2:17)

SEEING VISIONS AND DREAMING DREAMS

Then the LORD answered me and said: "Write the vision and make it plain on tablets, that he may run who reads it."

—Habakkuk 2:2 NKJV

_____
_____
_____
_____
_____
_____
_____
_____
_____
_____
_____
_____
_____
_____
_____
_____
_____
_____
_____
_____
_____
_____

SERVING THE VISION

And on My menservants and on My maidservants I will pour out
My Spirit in those days; and they shall prophesy.

—Acts 2:18 NKJV

This will be the second outpouring of the Holy Spirit. When He sets
His hand again for the second time, in full demonstration of His love,
power, and faithfulness, we take notice that the scripture says, "On 'my'
menservants and on 'my' maidservants," on male and female servants.

Knowing that we are "His" servants puts everything into proper
perspective. No matter what we do, we know that we are doing it for His
glory. Because the Holy Bible teaches us, saying, "And whatsoever ye
do, do it heartily, as to the Lord, and not unto men; knowing that of the
Lord ye shall receive the reward of the inheritance: for ye serve the Lord
Christ" (Colossians 3:23–24).

In His kingdom, the way up is down. "For whosoever exalteth
himself shall be abased; and he that humbleth himself shall be exalted"
(Luke 14:11).

> Likewise, ye younger, submit yourselves unto the elder.
> Yea, all of you be subject one to another, and be clothed
> with humility: for God resisteth the proud, and giveth

grace to the humble. Humble yourselves therefore under the mighty hand of God, that he may exalt you in due time. (1 Peter 5:5–6)

He is going to pour out His Spirit on His servants; that's going to happen. The question is, "Are we ready to get down on our knees? Are we ready to gird our waists as our Master did when He washed His disciples' feet?" After Jesus washed their feet, He taught them, saying, "For I have given you an example, that ye should do as I have done to you" (John 13:15). Our Jesus is the perfect example which we, as His servants and disciples, are to follow.

Everyone (for the most part) deep inside wants to be first, wants to win, and do great things. People want to see their visions come to pass, but are they willing to pay the price? Jesus discloses the recipe, but will we follow it? He said,

And whoever of you desires to be first shall be slave of all. For even the Son of Man did not come to be served, but to serve, and to give His life a ransom for many. (Mark 10:44–45 NKJV)

He also added,

But he that is greatest among you shall be your servant. (Matthew 23:11)

Do we want to be first? Do we want to be great? Do we want to be disciples of Jesus Christ and thus be like Him? Then we must start serving. This means that we are to serve somebody besides ourselves. We are to serve God by helping His children "grow up into him in all things, which is the head, even Christ" (Ephesians 4:15).

If and when we take care of His business, He will, in turn, simultaneously take care of ours. The Holy Bible says, "The LORD will perfect that which concerneth me" (Psalm 138:8), and we cannot forget this one, which we are so familiar with: "But seek ye first the kingdom of God, and his righteousness; and all these things shall be added unto you" (Matthew 6:33). Will we trust and apply the process?

Jesus Himself told us that He did not come to be served but to serve. This tells us that there is something very special about serving; there's something beautiful that happens through this action, which is difficult to discern with the modern eye. Serving fosters ongoing discipline. This is not a once-or-twice thing but one that happens every day. It is an attitude, a spirit. It's a lifestyle. It is through this lifestyle of serving, training, and practicing (doing) that we become like our Master. As we imitate, emulate, and assimilate Him, walk in Him, and surrender our lives to Him, He is then seen through us. Christlikeness and I'll keep saying it, "Christ in you, the hope of glory!" (Colossians 1:27).

Who did Jesus serve? First, He served the Father, then God's children. Our Master told us that He emulated the Father:

> Then answered Jesus and said unto them, Verily, verily,
> I say unto you, The Son can do nothing of himself, but
> what he seeth the Father do: for what things soever he
> doeth, these also doeth the Son likewise. (John 5:19)

All the great men and women of the Holy Bible served their leader or leaders, and they all became like them or greater. For example, we see that Moses served his father-in-law, Jethro.

> Now Moses kept the flock of Jethro his father in law,
> the priest of Midian: and he led the flock to the backside
> of the desert, and came to the mountain of God, even to
> Horeb. (Exodus 3:1)

Moses began serving by leading sheep in the middle of nowhere, and he ended up being used mightily as the shepherd of God.

> Then he remembered the days of old, Moses, and his people, saying, Where is he that brought them up out of the sea with the shepherd of his flock? where is he that put his holy Spirit within him? That led them by the right hand of Moses with his glorious arm, dividing the water before them, to make himself an everlasting name? that led them through the deep, as an horse in the wilderness, that they should not stumble? (Isaiah 63:11–13)

This pattern, as we shall see, is repeated many times throughout the scripture.

Joshua took orders from Moses and led the battle against Amalek.

> And Moses said unto Joshua, Choose us out men, and go out, fight with Amalek: to morrow I will stand on the top of the hill with the rod of God in mine hand. So Joshua did as Moses had said to him, and fought with Amalek: and Moses, Aaron, and Hur went up to the top of the hill. (Exodus 17:9–10)

By the way, he was victorious that day! "So Joshua defeated Amalek and his people with the edge of the sword" (Exodus 17:13 NKJV). He began by being Moses's assistant and ended up being chosen by God to continue where the prophet left off. He was commissioned to take the children of Israel into the Promised Land.

> Now after the death of Moses the servant of the LORD it came to pass, that the LORD spake unto Joshua the

son of Nun, Moses' minister [assistant], saying, Moses my servant is dead; now therefore arise, go over this Jordan, thou, and all this people, unto the land which I do give to them, even to the children of Israel. (Joshua 1:1–2)

Here, too, it is seen with the prophet Samuel. When he was a young child, his mother dedicated him to the LORD, and Samuel himself served in the Tabernacle of the LORD under Eli the priest.

And the child Samuel ministered unto the LORD before Eli. And the word of the LORD was precious in those days; there was no open vision. (1 Samuel 3:1)

Samuel became a prophet of God and a prominent figure in the Holy Bible. Samuel is the prophet who was sent to anoint King David. Samuel went through the motions, as everyone else did, and we are no exception. He learned through experience. He developed and advanced, "and the child Samuel grew on, and was in favour both with the LORD, and also with men" (1 Samuel 2:26).

It is through the act of serving that we are groomed for our calling. For the past thirteen and a half years, I've been serving and working for the LORD in the shadows, where nobody could see but Him. This whole time, I've been studying the Holy Bible and putting messages together to feed His flock, and now, out of nowhere (actually out of heaven), my Heavenly Father has enabled me to write this small (mustard seed–sized) book. My voice will now be heard and go beyond these walls. I can now see that He was preparing me this whole time.

And Samuel grew, and the LORD was with him, and did let none of his words fall to the ground. And all Israel from Dan even to Beersheba knew that Samuel was established to be a prophet of the LORD. And

the LORD appeared again in Shiloh: for the LORD revealed himself to Samuel in Shiloh by the word of the
LORD. (1 Samuel 3:19–21)

These men of God didn't stay there while they were serving man.
God was preparing them for something greater. So were they ever even
serving man to begin with? It is always our God "Who will render to
every man according to his deeds" (Romans 2:6) in the present time and
in that which is to come.

King David also served. This is the king who took Israel from being a little mouse that hides in the clefts of the rocks to becoming a roar-
ing lion that roams in the open fields of battle. When the prophet Samuel
went to the house of Jesse to anoint one of his sons, King David was
out of sight because he was busy serving. God had His eye on David,
though, and He always keeps His gaze fixed on his servants, ready to
stand up for them. "For the eyes of the LORD run to and fro throughout
the whole earth, to shew himself strong in the behalf of **them** whose
heart is perfect toward him" (2 Chronicles 16:9, emphasis added). God
sees a servant's loyal heart!

Then Jesse made Shammah to pass by. And he said,
Neither hath the LORD chosen this. Again, Jesse made
seven of his sons to pass before Samuel. And Samuel
said unto Jesse, The LORD hath not chosen these. And
Samuel said unto Jesse, Are here all thy children? And
he said, There remaineth yet the youngest, and, behold,
he keepeth the sheep. And Samuel said unto Jesse, Send
and fetch him: for we will not sit down till he come
hither. And he sent, and brought him in. Now he was
ruddy, and withal of a beautiful countenance, and good-
ly to look to. And the LORD said, Arise, anoint him:
for this is he. Then Samuel took the horn of oil, and
anointed him in the midst of his brethren: and the Spirit

of the LORD came upon David from that day forward. So Samuel rose up, and went to Ramah. (1 Samuel 16:9–13)

"For my thoughts are not your thoughts, neither are your ways my ways, saith the LORD" (Isaiah 55:8). Common sense tells us that if we are out of sight, we are out of mind. That may be true in an earthly sense, but we are not of this world; we are children of God, and we belong to His kingdom!

When an evil, distressing spirit came upon and troubled King Saul, his servants sought a skillful man to play the harp so that the king would be made well. They thought of David, and they knew where to find him.

Wherefore Saul sent messengers unto Jesse, and said, Send me David thy son, which is with the sheep. And David came to Saul, and stood before him: and he loved him greatly; and he became his armourbearer. And Saul sent to Jesse, saying, Let David, I pray thee, stand before me; for he hath found favour in my sight. And it came to pass, when the evil spirit from God was upon Saul, that David took an harp, and played with his hand: so Saul was refreshed, and was made well, and the evil spirit departed from him. (1 Samuel 16:19 and 21–23)

"The king said, 'Send him your son David, who is with the sheep.'" David was known for his service and was associated with the sheep. Where is young David? "Oh, he is tending the sheep." And it was from that lowly position that promotion came to him over and over again.

Now young David finally made it. He was working within the palace, and did he let all of this go to his head? Not at all, for he continued being a shepherd. He would travel back and forth from the palace to his father's house.

But David occasionally went and returned from Saul to feed his father's sheep at Bethlehem. (1 Samuel 17:15 NKJV)

It was all those years of tending the sheep that prepared him for all that was coming. It was there that the hand of the LORD tested him through numerous obstacles. That's why when he was confronted with Goliath the giant, it was a piece of cake for him. He must have said in his spirit, "For they are bread for us" (Numbers 14:9). There stood the Philistines champion, putting fear over the whole camp of Israel daily, and David said, "I can take him!" It was through serving that he was enabled.

Experience is truly invaluable; it gives you the vision to predict and prophesy outcomes!

And David said to Saul, Let no man's heart fail because of him; thy servant will go and fight with this Philistine. And Saul said to David, Thou art not able to go against this Philistine to fight with him: for thou art but a youth, and he a man of war from his youth. And David said unto Saul, Thy servant kept his father's sheep, and there came a lion, and a bear, and took a lamb out of the flock: and I went out after him, and smote him, and delivered it out of his mouth: and when he arose against me, I caught him by his beard, and smote Him, and slew him. Thy servant slew both the lion and the bear: and this uncircumcised Philistine shall be as one of them, seeing he hath defied the armies of the living God. David said moreover, The LORD that delivered me out of the paw of the lion, and out of the paw of the bear, he will deliver me out of the hand of this Philistine. And Saul said unto David, Go, and the LORD be with thee. (1 Samuel 17:32–37)

Let's fast-forward. We now find David sitting on the throne as king, and all his enemies have been subdued. He was living on plush. And he then decided to build God a house (a temple), but God sent King David a message through Nathan the prophet that his son Solomon would be the one to build the temple. "He shall build me an house" (1 Chronicles 17:12).

> Now therefore thus shalt thou say unto **my servant David**, Thus saith the LORD of hosts, I took thee from the sheepcote, even from following the sheep, that thou shouldest be ruler over my people Israel: and I have been with thee withersoever thou hast walked, and have cut off all thine enemies from before thee, and have made thee a name like the name of the great men that are in the earth. (1 Chronicles 17:7–8, emphasis added)

Furthermore,

> And it shall come to pass, when thy days be expired that thou must go to be with thy fathers, that I will raise up thy seed after thee, which shall be of thy sons; and I will establish his kingdom... According to all these words, and according to all this vision, so did Nathan speak unto David. (1 Chronicles 17:11 and 15)

"'I' took you from the sheepfold." It wasn't the prophet, not the king, not the good aim, or his good looks. It was not even good luck. God was the One who made David great. And He can do the same with us. Exaltation comes from the Lord.

Isn't that beautiful? I have personalized and prophesied that scripture over my life and over my future. "Jesse, I took you from the sheepfold." I visualize it, and I meditate on it. I think back on how I would risk my life on and for the streets that I grew up on without hesitation and how I gave it my all without reservation. I also genuinely loved my peers, especially the younger ones. They were like my family, my little brothers, and I had a responsibility, a duty, and a commitment to protect them. I know full well that my former lifestyle was wrong, but God can use anyone. One day, He pulled me out of all that and said, "Now you shall tend sheep for the kingdom!"

Serving is a "heart thing." David was chosen over his seven brothers, who might have been more qualified than him in certain aspects. I don't doubt that. However, God doesn't look at that. He doesn't see as a man sees. Man will look at someone and shake their head, saying, "There's no hope whatsoever for that person." God looks at your heart and says, "There's hope in your future," and, "By the way, you work for the King of kings now."

> But the LORD said unto Samuel, Look not on his countenance, or on the height of his stature; because I have refused him: for the LORD seeth not as man seeth; for man looketh on the outward appearance, but the LORD looketh on the heart. (1 Samuel 16:7)

God says, "And on My menservants and on My maidservants I will pour out My Spirit in those days" (Acts 2:18 NKJV). The question is, "Who was the Father's greatest servant?" It was Jesus Christ. We all know that. "My" servants is an endearing term that He uses as He makes claim over us. We are His business, but is He ours? Are we busy serving?

At twelve years old, we observe Jesus already redeeming the time by serving. Remember when His parents couldn't find Him?

> And He said to them, "Why did you seek Me? Did you not know that I must be about My Father's business?" (Luke 2:49 NKJV)

Our Heavenly Father holds a special place in His heart for the abused, the downcast, and the brokenhearted. That's why we are going to be surprised to see who He is going to use in this upcoming world-wide revival.

> For ye see your calling, brethren, how that not many wise men after the flesh, not many mighty, not many noble, are called: but God hath chosen the foolish things of the world to confound the wise; and God hath chosen the weak things of the world to confound the things which are mighty; and base things of the world, and things which are despised, hath God chosen, yea, and things which are not, to bring to nought things that are: that no flesh should glory in his presence. (1 Corinthians 1:26–29)

Jesus said, "But many that are first shall be last; and the last shall be first" (Matthew 19:30). God knows who's who and who's doing what, and that's what matters. Our serving is never in vain because it's done unto Him. That's why it says in the scriptures,

> But when you do a charitable deed, do not let your left hand know what your right hand is doing, that your charitable deed may be in secret; and your Father who sees in secret will Himself reward you openly. (Matthew 6:3–4 NKJV)

And that which is to be revealed shall be revealed! We are in the last days. We've been in the last days for over two thousand years (Hebrews 1:1–2; 1 Peter 4:7; 1 John 2:18). The last days began with Jesus Christ, although some like to place their finger on the day of Pentecost and say that is when the last days began. Either way, what is nonnegotiable is that we are in the last days right now. We are down to the last prophecies that need to be fulfilled—not many—for the second coming of our Lord and Savior Jesus Christ. I repeat the words of the prophet Martin Luther King Jr. in response to the outcry of the masses: "How long? Not long!"

Interestingly, one of the prophecies that is soon to come is a massive transfer of wealth. It shall be granted, rendered, and paid back to the servants of God.

> Go to now, ye rich men, weep and howl for your miseries that shall come upon you. Your riches are corrupted, and your garments are motheaten. Your gold and silver is cankered; and the rust of them shall be a witness against you, and shall eat your flesh as it were fire. **Ye have heaped treasure together for the last days**. Behold, the hire of the labourers who have reaped down your fields, which is of you kept back by fraud, crieth: and the cries of them which have reaped are entered into the ears of the Lord of sabaoth. Ye have lived in pleasure on the earth, and been in wanton; ye have nourished your hearts, as in a day of slaughter. Ye have condemned and killed the just; and he doth not resist you. (James 5:1–6, emphasis added)

The Lord of Sabaoth means "the Lord of hosts" or "the Lord of the armies." God is our defender, and He is in control, regardless of how dim the situation may look.

A rich man can look down from his balcony, overseeing his whole estate, which is surrounded by vineyards. He then observes one of his laborers, hunched over with sweat dripping from his brow, from sun up until sundown. What the owner can't see is whose child this worker is and the vision that he has in his heart. One day, the Spirit of God says to His servant, "Look up, you see that high balcony? You shall be there soon, and all this shall be yours, and more, but never forget the small people, where you yourself once came from." This scenario reminds me of two kings who lost their kingdoms in the Holy Bible.

King Saul,

> And Samuel said unto him, The LORD hath rent the kingdom of Israel from thee this day, and hath given it to a neighbour of thine, that is better than thou. (1 Samuel 15:28)

And King Nebuchadnezzar,

> The king spake, and said, Is not this great Babylon, that I have built for the house of the kingdom by the might of my power, and for the honour of my majesty? While the word was in the king's mouth, there fell a voice from heaven, saying, O king Nebuchadnezzar, to thee it is spoken; The kingdom is departed from thee. (Daniel 4:30–31)

Both of these kings lost their kingdoms by the Word of the Lord by way of His doing.

> LORD maketh poor, and maketh rich: he bringeth low, and lifteth up. He raiseth up the poor out of the dust, and lifteth up the beggar from the dunghill, to set them among princes, and to make them inherit the throne of glory: for the pillars of the earth are the LORD's and he hath set the world upon them. (1 Samuel 2:7–8)

Serving doesn't always come easy; however, it does yield a good reward. Not only a spiritual one but a tangible one as well. For the character and posture that a servant develops are of great necessity in this age and time. The trades, wisdom, and spirit are transferable. It is a fact that your leader's traits will rub off on you, as we see that they did on Jesus's apostles.

> Now when they saw the boldness of Peter and John, and perceived that they were uneducated and untrained men, they marveled. And they realized that they had been with Jesus. (Acts 4:13 NKJV)

Serving and following Jesus Christ go hand in hand. By doing both, we thus step into His ministry and are empowered by the Father, causing Him to move through us.

> If any man serve me, let him follow me; and where I am, there shall also my servant be: if any man serve me, him will my Father honour. (John 12:26)

Jesus posed a question to His disciples and answered it for them. He said,

> For who is greater, he who sits at the table, or he who serves? Is it not he who sits at the table? Yet I am among you as the One who serves. But you are those who have continued with Me in My trials. And I bestow upon you a kingdom, just as My Father bestowed one upon Me. (Luke 22:27–29 NKJV).

Though serving tables can be a figure of speech, it is indicative in the scripture that Jesus is personally serving His disciples, and He takes advantage of a good teaching opportunity. What better than an in-your-face, in-the-moment personal illustration? At first glance, serving tables may seem like a menial task, yet this act of ministry is what served as a springboard for Stephen, the first martyr. He began by waiting on tables, and a few verses later, we see God working miracles through him.

> And in those days, when the number of the disciples was multiplied, there arose a murmuring of the Grecians against the Hebrews, because their widows were neglected in the daily ministration. Then the twelve called the multitude of the disciples unto them, and said, It is not reason that we should leave the word of God, and serve tables. Wherefore, brethren, look ye out among you seven men of honest report, full of the Holy Ghost and wisdom, whom we may appoint over this business. But we will give ourselves continually to prayer, and to the ministry of the word. And the saying pleased the whole multitude: and they chose Stephen, a man full of faith and of the Holy Ghost, and Philip, and Prochorus, and Nicanor, and Timon, and Parmenas, and Nicolas a proselyte of Antioch: whom they set before the apostles: and when they had prayed, they laid their hands on them. And the word of God increased; and the number of the disciples multiplied in Jerusalem greatly; and a great company of the priests were obedient to the faith. And Stephen, full of faith and power, did great wonders and miracles among the people. (Acts 6:1–8)

What if Stephen would've said, "I'm sorry, but I'm too experienced for this," or, "Serve tables? Oh, no, not me. There's no future in that," do you think that he would've been as impactful? Probably not, but because of his humble spirit, he went on to give one of the longest and most meticulous sermons recorded in the Holy Bible. The whole chapter 7 of the book of Acts is pretty much devoted to his discourse. It is said that his preaching was so moving that Jesus Christ, Who is seated at the right hand of the Father, stood up to His feet and gave Stephen a standing ovation as he was being received up in glory!

> But he, being full of the Holy Ghost, looked up sted-
> fastly into heaven, and saw the glory of God, and Jesus
> standing on the right hand of God, and said, Behold, I
> see the heavens opened, and the Son of man standing
> on the right hand God... And they stoned Stephen, call-
> ing upon God, and saying, Lord Jesus, receive my spir-
> it. And he kneeled down, and cried with a loud voice,
> Lord, lay not this sin to their charge. And when he had
> said this, he fell asleep. (Acts 7:55–56 and 59–60)

You see, a lot of saints want to start off by preaching, but most preachers, evangelists, pastors, and teachers will reveal that they began by serving, and only then was the door opened. They will also disclose that they have never really stopped serving. The servant of God never retires.

We are His instruments here on earth, and our Heavenly Father uses man in His immense work of salvation. For it is written, "And this gospel of the kingdom shall be preached in all the world for a witness unto all nations; and then shall the end come" (Matthew 24:14). That preaching (witnessing) is going to be accomplished by the Holy Spirit, operating through His servants. Jesus pronounced to every generation, "The harvest truly is plenteous, but the labourers are few; pray ye there-fore the Lord of the harvest, that he will send forth labourers into his harvest" (Matthew 9:37–38).

We are the "servants and laborers," but this is "His" harvest. The mission of the great commission has not changed. After Jesus's death and resurrection, the Great Commission of global evangelism and disci-pleship was carried on by His apostles and, afterward, by the believers who would succeed them from generation to generation all the way up until the end of the age.

> And Jesus came and spoke to them, saying, "All au-
> thority has been given to Me in heaven and on earth. Go
> therefore and make disciples of all the nations, baptiz-
> ing them in the name of the Father and of the Son and of
> the Holy Spirit, teaching them to observe all things that
> I have commanded you; and lo, I am with you always,
> even to the end of the age." Amen. (Matthew 28:18–20
> NKJV)

When Jesus was walking the earth and His hour was approaching, a high priest by the name of Caiaphas, under the inspiration of the Holy Spirit, gave a prophecy pertaining to and revealing the purpose of our Savior's death.

> And one of them, named Caiaphas, being the high priest
> that same year, said unto them, Ye know nothing at all,
> nor consider that it is expedient for us, that one man
> should die for the people, and that the whole nation per-
> ish not. And this spake he not of himself: but being high
> priest that year, he prophesied that Jesus should die for
> that nation; and not for that nation only, but that also he
> should gather together in one the children of God that
> were scattered abroad. (John 11:49–52)

Let's emphasize the last verse: "And not for that nation only, but that also he should gather together in one the children of God that were scattered abroad" (John 11:52). This part—of reaching those who are scattered abroad—is to be accomplished through our faithful service unto Him, and that's why "our Heavenly Father needs us." Jesus self-lessly died on our behalf so that we may be saved and live a life eternal. My brothers and sisters, will we, in turn, show our "gratitude and appre-ciation" by laboring for Him? Will we go out and serve in His kingdom?

The wisdom of the book of Proverbs tells us, "He who tills his land will have plenty of bread, but he who follows frivolity will have poverty enough!" (Proverbs 28:19 NKJV). Does this not also apply to "kingdom business" and our vision? Those who till, labor, and serve for the Lord will have plenty! And according to Proverbs, we are candidates to receive even more: "The wealth of the sinner is laid up for the just" (Proverbs 13:22). And then there's "he that by usury and unjust gain increaseth his substance, he shall gather it for him that will pity the poor" (Proverbs 28:8). The financing lies with the Lord, so if you could do "whatever" or "anything" in serving the kingdom and money wasn't an issue, what would it be (biblically speaking)?

Make room because it's coming, given that you know what you want, have written the vision, have asked the Father, and are taking action steps toward it. "For faith without works is dead." Are we asking on behalf and for the benefit of the body of Christ and for the glory of the Father?

Make room, dig ditches, and prepare yourself to receive and do whatever it takes so that God's hand can freely move through your life.

> Enlarge the place of thy tent, and let them stretch forth the curtains of thine habitations: spare not, lengthen thy cords, and strengthen thy stakes; for thou shalt break forth on the right hand and on the left; and thy seed shall inherit the Gentiles, and make the desolate cities to be inhabited. (Isaiah 54:2–3)

Take your limits off God. He is the Almighty! He is talking about your vision. It's time to augment it! Like an image on your smartphone that you can magnify and broaden by "widening" and "extending" your fingertips on the screen of your life. Yes, your imagination! Enlarge it, stretch it, do not spare it, and lengthen it! Do not hold back, for God shall bestow on you in accordance with the volume of your vision, in proportion to the level of your petitions, and consistent with what you ask, and you will only ask for what you can see. (Get in your Word!)

> Ask of Me, and I will give You the nations for Your in-
> heritance, and the ends of the earth for Your possession.
> (Psalm 2:8 NKJV)

Our Heavenly Father knows that sometimes we feel like there's nothing left, and our spirit wanes. But that's when we must keep going and continue fighting. Menservants and maidservants, we must proceed, for we shall doubtlessly receive His increase! I already see the first ray of sunlight; it's morning, and with it comes joy. "They that sow in tears shall reap in joy" (Psalm 126:5)—they that sow the good seed, the Word.

> Sow to yourselves in righteousness, reap in mercy;
> break up your fallow ground: for it is time to seek the
> LORD, till he come and rain righteousness upon you.
> (Hosea 10:12)

There is another contrast that I want us to focus on between verses 17 and 18 of Acts chapter 2. In verse 17, it mentions "seeing visions and dreaming dreams," while in verse 18, it doesn't include that; it just says, "And they shall prophesy." Does that mean that in the second out-pouring, we won't see visions or dream dreams? Not at all. "Dreaming dreams and seeing visions" will be included, if anything, all the more!

The prophetic comes with the territory. Nonetheless, let us not forget that the first outpouring of the Holy Spirit occurred when the church was birthed and filled with power. We also bear in mind that at that point in time, they did not have the complete Book of the Holy Bible, from Genesis all the way through to Revelation. Especially for them, the book of Acts and all of the epistles of Paul and of the other apostles that teach us so much on church doctrine, how a church is to be built and overseen, and what it is to be a Christian. Therefore, they depended on the Old Testament scriptures and the writings and words of the apostles. Of which writings and words were equated in authority to the Old Testament scriptures. The words of the apostles carried great weight. We are going to see how the apostle Peter compares Paul's epistles and puts them on the same level with the Old Testament scriptures, which everyone at that time and now knows to be the very Word of God:

> As also in all his epistles, speaking in them of these things, in which are some things hard to understand, which untaught and unstable people twist to their own destruction, as they do also the rest of the Scriptures. (2 Peter 3:16 NKJV)

Paul also references and affirms his and the apostles' message as being the Living Word of God and not the word of men:

> For this cause also thank we God without ceasing, because, when ye received the word of God which ye heard of us, ye received it not as the word of men, but as it is in truth, the word of God, which effectually worketh also in you that believe. (1 Thessalonians 2:13)

The early church also relied on the visions and dreams that they received from God, as He was leading them through His Spirit. This was not only limited to the leadership; the Gentiles were also receiving visions from God.

> There was a certain man in Caesarea called Cornelius, a centurion of the band called the Italian band, a devout man, and one that feared God with all his house, which gave much alms to the people, and prayed to God

always. He saw in a vision evidently about the ninth
hour of the day an angel of God coming in to him, and
saying unto him, Cornelius. And when he looked on
him, he was afraid, and said, What is it Lord? And he
said unto him, Thy prayers and thine alms are come up
for a memorial before God. (Acts 10:1–4)

The apostles Paul and Peter had visions and dreams all the time. It
was also through visions that the apostle John received the whole book
of Revelation on the island of Patmos.

Today, we have the complete Book, and we can wholly rely on it.
"All scripture is given by inspiration of God, and is profitable for doctrine, for reproof, for correction, for instruction in righteousness: that the
man of God may be perfect, throughly furnished unto all good works"
(2 Timothy 3:16–17).

The Holy Bible is the blueprint from which we receive instruction
and pattern our whole life after. It holds all things that pertain to life
and godliness. Yes, our God can personally give you or show you a sign
through one or many visions or dreams that shall never cease. Yet at the
end of the day, and being that we are in the last days, it is the Word of
God that the menservants and the maidservants of today are to hearken
to, follow, and prophesy. And everything else that we say "must" line up
with His Word and His Spirit. In other words, there must be agreement
and harmony between our vision, our dreams, our prophecies, and what
the Word says.

The apostle Paul said it best:

But though we, or an angel from heaven, preach any
other gospel unto you than that which we have preached
unto you, let him be accursed. (Galatians 1:8)

We are instructed, for our own good, to "test all things; hold fast what is good" (1 Thessalonians 5:21 NKJV). Does what I am reading, hearing, and seeing line up? The apostle John also gives a warning:

> Beloved, believe not every spirit, but try the spirits whether they are of God: because many false prophets are gone out into the world. (1 John 4:1)

As it has been previously mentioned, we are not waiting for the Holy Spirit to return, for He never left. We are waiting for the second outpouring, for the second shower. The apostle Peter said on the day of Pentecost,

> For the promise is unto you, and to your children, and to all that are afar off, even as many as he Lord our God shall call. (Acts 2:39)

The promise of the Spirit is to all who are far off, into the future, and who will believe. The Holy Bible also tells us to be filled with the Spirit! However, when our Heavenly Father fills us, His manifestations begin to happen in supernatural fashion. There's wine, and then there's the new wine, the good wine, the strong stuff.

> Jesus saith unto them, Fill the waterpots with water. And they filled them up to the brim. (John 2:7)

Do you believe that it is the Father's good pleasure for His servants to be filled to the brim? On that day, we shall personally experience the true meaning of "my cup runneth over."

The Holy Spirit pointed out "signs" (miracles) in the book of Acts 2:19: "Signs in the earth beneath." These signs are mentioned after the outpourings mentioned in the two previous verses (v. 17 and v. 18). Why did God inspire Peter to prophesy signs in the middle of the prophecy? Because God knew that this account would be documented by Luke, that you and I would take notice—along with many other believers, and that we would believe His Word. If it says that the church is going to have and perform miracles, then there are going to be miracles—period. This prophecy expands from the day of Pentecost all the way to its completion at the end of the millennial reign of Christ. The millennial reign is when we shall live and reign with Jesus on earth for a thousand years (Revelation 20:4). Then comes the judgment (Revelation 20:11–15). And thus, the era of "the Last Days" will end.

The Spirit of God set up the following order for the church through the apostle Paul:

> Now ye are the body of Christ, and members in particular. And God hath set some in the church, first apostles, secondarily prophets, thirdly teachers, after that miracles, then gifts of healings, helps, governments, diversities of tongues. Are all apostles? are all prophets? are all teachers? **are all workers of miracles?** (1 Corinthians 12:27–29, emphasis added)

Here, Jesus is explaining to His disciples the workings of the Holy Spirit:

> He that hath my commandments, and keepeth them, he it is that loveth me: and he that loveth me shall be loved of my Father, and I will love him, and will manifest myself to him. (John 14:21)

And when God shows and manifests Himself through His Spirit, He can display His potency as He sees fit through His established order. Let's remember that He is God. He can do anything. If He used a donkey to talk in the Old Testament (Numbers 22:20–34), He can use any willing vessel.

I have heard the naysayers say that the miracles were only for the early church in the book of Acts, but that's absurd because God does not change. "For I am the LORD, I change not" (Malachi 3:6). Miracles have been happening since the beginning of time, and they will continue until the end! We see miracles taking place in the book of Revelation; this is a scene that will take place in the future:

> And I will give power unto my two witnesses, and they shall prophesy a thousand two hundred and threescore days, clothed in sackcloth. These are the two olive trees, and the two candlesticks standing before the God of the earth. And if any man will hurt them, fire proceedeth out of their mouth, and devoureth their enemies: and if any man will hurt them, he must in this manner be killed. These have power to shut heaven, that it rain not in the days of their prophecy: and have power over waters to turn them to blood, and to smite the earth with all plagues, as often as they will. (Revelation 11:3–6)

"Fire proceeds from their mouth, and they have the power to turn the waters to blood and to strike the earth with plagues? Jesse, is there something less drastic, like a little more conventional?"

"Yes, there is."

The apostle James tells us in his Epistle,

> Is any sick among you? let him call for the elders of the church; and let them pray over him, anointing him with oil in the name of the Lord: and the prayer of faith shall save the sick, and the Lord shall raise him up; and if he have committed sins, they shall be forgiven him. Confess your faults one to another, and pray one for another,

that ye may be healed. The effectual fervent prayer of a righteous man availeth much. (James 5:14–16)

We serve a mighty God. It is our role and responsibility to pray, prophesy His Word, and lay hands on the sick, and the Father does the rest of the work. He performs healings, signs, and wonders. Who are we, or who is anybody, to tell God how to operate? This is who God is and how He testifies. "God also bearing them witness, both with signs and wonders, and with divers miracles, and gifts of the Holy Ghost, according to his own will" (Hebrews 2:4).

My fellow Bereans, fine "servants" of the kingdom, we have learned a lot. Rest assured that we have not been drinking baby milk; together, we have partaken of the type of spiritual nutrition that it speaks about in Hebrews.

For every one that useth milk is unskilful in the word of righteousness: for he is a babe. But strong meat belongeth to them that are of full age, even those who by reason of use have their senses exercised to discern both good and evil. (Hebrews 5:13–14)

The more we apply what we have learned, the stronger our spirit man gets! "By reason of use" is equal to "being of service," and being of service is a perfect opportunity to train and grow.

May the Holy Spirit always remind us of the following:

And whatsoever ye do in word or deed, do all in the name of the Lord Jesus, giving thanks to God and the Father by him. (Colossians 3:17)

SERVING THE VISION

Then the LORD answered me and said: "Write the vision and make it plain on tablets, that he may run who reads it."

—Habakkuk 2:2 NKJV

_____

_____

_____

_____

_____

_____

_____

_____

_____

_____

_____

_____

_____

_____

_____

_____

_____

_____

CHAPTER 23

THE VISION OF THE LORD'S HARVEST

In the Old Testament, in the days of old (and it still holds true today), when the crops physically received the former rain and the latter rain, it meant that the people would be able to move to gather in the wheat and the grain. Their vats would be filled with new wine and oil. It would end up being a good harvest, and the land would overflow with bread (Joel 2:23–24).

In the same way, in the New Testament and today, in the ongoing "Acts of the church," when we receive the rain of the Holy Spirit, we get the "works, signs, and wonders." Not to mention the fruits: "But the fruit of the Spirit is love, joy, peace, longsuffering, gentleness, goodness, faith, meekness, temperance: against such there is no law" (Galatians 5:22–23). If we received that on the former rain, how much more can we expect on the latter rain?

We, the children of God, are the harvest! Jesus taught us, saying,

> Most assuredly, I say to you, unless a grain of wheat
> falls into the ground and dies, it remains alone; but if it
> dies, it produces much grain. (John 12:24 NKJV)

Much "grain" literally means much "fruit." Jesus is speaking of Himself and of reproducing Himself as a result of gathering in many sons on the day of His revealing—the day of the harvest.

When and how will this event take place? The Holy Bible has a lot to say about the Father bringing in many sons to glory. This is a day that we eagerly await. Let's turn to the scriptures.

> For it became him, for whom are all things, and by whom are all things, in bringing many sons unto glory, to make the captain of their salvation perfect through sufferings. (Hebrews 2:10)

Jesus will bring in many sons to glory by glorifying Himself in His saints!

> When he shall come to be glorified in his saints, and to be admired in all them that believe (because our testimony among you was believed) in that day. (2 Thessalonians 1:10)

On that day, it won't be us training to be like Jesus; on that day, we will be completely transformed to be like Jesus—not our doing, but His doing. I'll let the Word explain it.

> For we know that if our earthly house of this tabernacle were dissolved, we have a building of God, an house not made with hands, eternal in the heavens. For in this we groan, earnestly desiring to be clothed upon with our house which is from heaven: if so be that being clothed we shall not be found naked. For we that are in this tabernacle do groan, being burdened: not for that we would

be unclothed, but clothed upon, that mortality might be swallowed up of life. (2 Corinthians 5:1–4)

Even the whole creation (creature) awaits this day, for it, too, shall get a piece of the action! (And one day, too, there will be a new earth (Revelation 21:1).)

And if children, then heirs; heirs of God, and joint-heirs with Christ; if so be that we suffer with him, that we may be also glorified together. For I reckon that the sufferings of this present time are not worthy to be compared with the glory which shall be revealed in us. For the earnest expectation of the creature waiteth for the **manifestation** of the sons of God. For we know that the whole creation groaneth and travaileth in pain together until now. And not only they, but ourselves also, which have the first fruits of the Spirit, even we ourselves groan within ourselves, waiting for the adoption, to wit, the redemption of our body. (Romans 8:17–19 and 22–23, emphasis added)

The apostle Paul further reassures us in detail of this glorious day:

But I would not have you to be ignorant, brethren, concerning them which are asleep, that ye sorrow not, even as others which have no hope. For if we believe that Jesus died and rose again, even so them also which sleep in Jesus will God bring with him. For this we say unto you by the word of the Lord, that we which are alive and remain unto the coming of the Lord shall not prevent them which are asleep. For the Lord himself shall descend from heaven with a shout, with the voice of the archangel, and with the trump of God: and the dead in Christ shall rise first: then we which are alive and remain shall be caught up together with them in the clouds, to meet the Lord in the air: and so shall we ever be with the Lord. Wherefore comfort one another with these words. (1 Thessalonians 4:13–18)

The apostle John, during his old age and while in exile on the island of Patmos, saw this harvest taking place through the vision that was given to him by Jesus Christ, which was written in the book of Revelation.

And I looked, and behold a white cloud, and upon the cloud one sat like unto the Son of man, having on his head a golden crown, and in his hand a sharp sickle. And another angel came out of the temple, crying with a loud voice to him that sat on the cloud, Thrust in thy sickle, and reap: for the time is come for thee to reap; for the harvest of the earth is ripe. And he that sat on the cloud thrust in his sickle on the earth; and the earth was reaped. (Revelation 14:14–16)

One day, we shall have a body like the celestial and spiritual body of Jesus Christ.

Beloved, now are we the sons of God, and it doth not yet appear what we shall be: but we know that, when he shall appear, we shall be like him; for we shall see him as he is. (1 John 3:2)

You may have heard it said that "we are not human beings having a spiritual experience, but we are spiritual beings having an earthly human experience." Yes, we are no longer of this world; we are just pilgrims and sojourners passing through.

THE LITTLE SEED

This is scripture. This is the truth; it is the word of God, which means that through it, God Himself has told us that "we will be like Him, like Jesus!" We will not be a "type and a shadow" or a "pattern," but we shall be an "actual" in bodily form.

So how do we know that there is going to be a "latter rain" of the outpouring of the Holy Spirit? Because the Holy Bible says that, in the end-time, God is going to bring in a great harvest! And every harvest, according to the scripture, by natural and spiritual principle, has two rain seasons.

> Let us know, let us pursue the knowledge of the LORD.
> His going forth is established as the morning; He will
> come to us like the rain, like the latter and former rain
> to the earth. (Hosea 6:3 NKJV)

The knowledge of the Lord in this given topic is that He has established and appointed seasons, a former rain and a latter rain. He has also reserved the latter rain, which He shall faithfully render to us, the church.

> Neither say they in their heart, Let us now fear the
> LORD our God, that giveth rain, both the former and
> the latter, in his season: he reserveth unto us the ap-
> pointed weeks of the harvest. (Jeremiah 5:24)

The season of the latter rain will come before the harvest of the LORD. And the latter rain is what will fill and fuel the church, causing it to go out and mass evangelize in fulfillment of the prophecy that says, "Until the fulness of the Gentiles be come in" (Romans 11:25). Once that specific number is completed, which only God knows, and the blindness is removed from Israel (the Jewish people), then the harvest of the earth will be ripe, and then He will reap the earth!

Remember, my Bereans, sons of the kingdom, whether today, tomorrow, or in those days of mass revival, it is always our Heavenly Father Who does the works through the Holy Spirit. And "greater works" will He do through us because we shall believe and ask in an unprecedented manner and with all boldness!

THE VISION OF THE LORD'S HARVEST

Then the LORD answered me and said: "Write the vision and make it plain on tablets, that he may run who reads it."

—Habakkuk 2:2 NKJV

THE VISION OF ONE ACCORD

Since the latter rain is what quickens the Lord's harvest, then how do we trigger or call upon it, hence bringing down the second outpouring of the Holy Spirit? Thank God that we have His Word to answer all our questions. The Holy Bible is our roadmap to life.

The scripture tells us that we are to specifically pray for the rain in the time of the latter rain. And that the LORD will answer with flashing clouds! Here in the book of Zechariah, we will see that it does not say, "The former and the latter rain," as it does in other passages. Why wasn't the former rain mentioned? Because I believe that this scripture is prophetically pointing to the second outpouring of the Holy Spirit. The prophet prophesied,

> Ask the LORD for rain in the time of the latter rain. The LORD will make flashing clouds; He will give them showers of rain, grass in the field for everyone. (Zechariah 10:1 NKJV)

We are told to pray for rain in the time of the latter rain. When will that time be? The Word of God says,

> For thus saith the LORD Of hosts; Yet once, **it is a little
> while**, and I will shake the heavens, and the earth, and
> the sea, and the dry land. (Haggai 2:6, emphasis added)

Yes, "it is a little while, and the heavens will be shaken." They shall be shaken in response to our prayer. The body of Christ is going to do something that has never been attempted in such extraordinary and un-precedented magnitude. "Our" goal (which is in alignment with Scrip-ture and the Spirit) is to unite the whole world for corporate prayer. In a church setting or congregation, corporate prayer means that the prayer is being performed by all the members (in communion and in agreement), which is synonymous with being in "one accord." Being in one accord, or in one agreement, brings to mind the idea of everybody doing some-thing "at the same time." Thus, the whole world, with one accord, at the same time, united in corporate prayer, praying for the same thing, "The latter rain of the Holy Spirit." Not a random prayer but specifically the scripture in the book of Isaiah that says,

> Oh that thou wouldest rend the heavens, that thou
> wouldest come down, that the mountains might flow
> down at thy presence. (Isaiah 64:1)

My brethren, within the reach of the Holy Spirit, all of us must unite and work together to make this happen. For we shall go up on the heavenly "hall of faith" (like the one spoken of in the book of Hebrews) as the generation of Christians who brought down the heavens! He who has an ear, let him hear.

To know how to embark upon this grand and marvelous assign-ment, we are going to have to turn to the Book. And we are going to look at the pattern that was laid down for us. We will use the book of Acts to see what we can learn from when the first outpouring took place. This is the account made by Luke, the physician, after the ascension of Jesus Christ:

> Then returned they unto Jerusalem from the mount called Olivet, which is from Jerusalem a sabbath day's journey. And when they were come in, they went up into an upper room, where abode both Peter, and James, and John, and Andrew, Philip, and Thomas, Bartholomew, and Matthew, James the son of Alphaeus, and Simon Zelotes, and Judas the brother of James. These all continued **with one accord** in prayer and supplication, with the women, and Mary the mother of Jesus, and with his brethren. (Acts 1:12–14, emphasis added)

Then,

> And when the day of Pentecost was fully come, they were all **with one accord** in one place. And suddenly there came a sound from heaven as of a rushing mighty wind, and it filled all the house where they were sitting. And there appeared unto them cloven tongues like as of fire, and it sat upon each of them. And they were all filled with the Holy Ghost, and began to speak with other tongues, as the Spirit gave them utterance. (Acts 2:1–4, emphasis added)

ME. So what do we see in these verses that we can apply to call upon the second outpouring of the Holy Spirit?

YOU. That they all continued with one accord in prayer and supplication, and they were filled with the Spirit, and they got fired up for the Lord!

ME. Correct. However, we can add one more thing that was not noted, and that is "the upper room."

Why is the upper room important? Because if they needed an upper room, then we are going to need one as well. Their upper room held

237

about a hundred and twenty disciples (Acts 1:15). "Anyone have any ideas? We need a place where we can fit entire cities, states, and continents full of people. We are talking about the whole world!"

This is where the awesomeness of God and His infinite wisdom reveals just how amazing He is! If the following doesn't blow you away, it's probably because your dynamite is wet or has no fuse. So we are looking for an upper room big enough to house the world. "I got it!" What we are really looking for is a structure, a "house, building, or temple!" Ring any bells?

Well, if you recall, back in chapter 4, "The Vision of Habakkuk," we learned that we are being built up a spiritual house and a building that grows into a temple. Let's refresh our spiritual minds for a moment:

> [The Son] To whom coming, as unto [The Father] a living stone, disallowed indeed of men, but chosen of God, and precious, ye also, as lively stones, are built up a **spiritual house**, an holy priesthood, to offer up spiritual sacrifices, acceptable to God by Jesus Christ. (1 Peter 2:4– 5, emphasis added)

And,

> In whom all the **building** fitly framed together groweth unto an holy **temple** in the Lord. (Ephesians 2:21, emphasis added)

Perhaps now it makes sense why God would build us and fit us together into a spiritual house. This house has a name; it is called "the Tabernacle of David," and it was reactivated on the day of Pentecost, and it was used during the first outpouring of the Holy Spirit to win souls for the kingdom. When mass numbers of Gentiles began receiving salvation (and the Holy Spirit), a discussion arose among the leaders. And it was confirmed that God did not make any distinction between Jews and Gentiles (Acts 15:8–11). Then the apostle James agreed and spoke the following in alignment with and in fulfillment of an Old Testament prophecy:

> And after they had held their peace, James answered, saying, Men and brethren, hearken unto me: Simeon hath declared how God at the first did visit the Gentiles, to take out of them a people for his name. And to this agree the words of the prophets; as it is written, **After this I will return, and will build again the tabernacle of David**, which is fallen down; and I will build again the ruins thereof, and I will set it up: that the residue of men might seek after the Lord, and all the Gentiles, upon whom my name is called, saith the Lord, who doeth all these things. Known unto God are all his works from the beginning of the world. (Acts 15:13–18, emphasis added)

The phrase that we just read, "And all the Gentiles, upon whom my name is called," in conjunction with a temple, brings to mind where it says, "If my people, which are called by my name, shall humble themselves, and pray, and seek my face, and turn from their wicked ways; then will I hear from heaven, and will forgive their sin, and will heal their land" (2 Chronicles 7:14). The LORD heard the prayer that King Solomon had made in dedication of the finished temple. In the next scripture, the word *house* literally means *temple*. We are going to discover something valuable here that will assist us in accomplishing our objective. While praying, King Solomon said,

> But will God in very deed dwell with men on the earth? behold, heaven and the heaven of heavens cannot contain thee; how much less this **house** which I have built! have respect therefore to the prayer of thy servant, and

to his supplication, O LORD my God, to hearken unto the cry and the prayer which thy servant prayeth before thee: that thine eyes may be open upon this **house** day and night, upon the place whereof thou hast said that thou wouldest put thy name there; to hearken unto the prayer which thy servant prayeth toward this place. Hearken therefore unto the supplications of thy servant, and of thy people Israel, **which they shall make toward this place**: hear thou from thy dwelling place, even from heaven; and when thou hearest, forgive. (2 Chronicles 6:18–21, emphasis added)

The priest, the king, and the people were to make "prayer and supplication" toward the temple, and God would hear them. Back then, in the times of physical temples, prayers and supplications were to be made in the temple or facing in the direction of the temple. Today, "the Tabernacle of David" is the spiritual temple, one made up of and comprised of living stones, and prayer is not made in the temple. The temple is the one doing the praying. And today, the people don't face a temple because the time has arrived when the living temple, "the Tabernacle of David," faces heaven (and speaks to heaven!). We lift up our eyes toward our Father.

We've found the house! We also already have the prayer, where we are asking Him, "Oh that thou wouldest rend the heavens, that thou wouldest come down!" But it does say, "Prayer and supplication." We need the supplications. We have that too! Let's read what the psalmist wrote:

Return, we beseech thee, O God of hosts: look down from heaven, and behold, and visit this vine; and the vineyard which thy right hand hath planted, and the branch that thou madest strong for thyself. It is burned with fire, it is cut down: they perish at the rebuke of thy countenance. Let thy hand be upon the man of thy right hand, upon the son of man whom thou madest strong for thyself. So will not we go back from thee: quicken us, and we will call upon thy name. Turn us again, O LORD God of hosts, cause thy face to shine; and we shall be saved. (Psalm 80:14–19)

The last phase is the one of being in "one accord," and then we shall be ready. One of the best examples of one accord can be found in the book of Genesis, where the people set out to build a city and a colossal tower that reached the heavens. The principles that they used are still applicable in today's day and time. And though God disagreed with their idea, plan, and project, He remarked in approval on the effectiveness of the method that they were using—a method that we shall utilize and incorporate for the vision of one accord. You see, they tried to reach the heavens, and we, on the other hand, are already there! "And hath raised us up together, and made us sit together in heavenly places in Christ Jesus" (Ephesians 2:6).

What we are going to do, under the authority of the scripture, is bring the heavens down! "Oh that thou wouldest rend the heavens, that thou wouldest come down!" Yes, Holy Father, "return, we beseech thee, O God of hosts: look down from heaven, and behold, and visit this vine."

In the book of Genesis, it is written,

And the whole earth was of one language, and of one speech. And it came to pass, as they journeyed from the east, that they found a plain in the land of Shinar; and they dwelt there. And they said one to another, Go to, let us make brick, and burn them throughly. And they had brick for stone, and slime had they for morter. And they said, Go to, let us build us a city and a tower, whose top may reach unto heaven; and let us make us a name, lest we be scattered abroad upon the face of the whole earth.

And the LORD came down to see the city and the tower, which the children of men builded. And the LORD said, Behold, **the people is one**, and they have all one language; and this they begin to do: **and now nothing will be restrained from them, which they have imagined to do**. Go to, let us go down, and there confound their language, that they may not understand one another's speech. So the LORD scattered them abroad from thence upon the face of all the earth: and they left off to build the city. Therefore is the name of it called Babel; because the LORD did there confound the language of all the earth: and from thence did the LORD scatter them abroad upon the face of all the earth. (Genesis 11:1–9, emphasis added)

And the LORD basically said, "Look, indeed the people are all one, they all have one language, and now this is what they begin to do, now nothing whatsoever which they have imagined to do shall be withheld from them." What was their secret? It was that they were of one accord. The people were one; they had one language, and they had one goal. They were all working together. In essence, God said "that by applying this formula, they would be successful in everything." So since they were in one accord with one another but in discord with the will of God, He "came down" and scattered them. They were confounded by different languages. We will be united by one name, the name of Jesus. God came down, and they were scattered. God will come down, and we will be watered, filled, and empowered!

A piece of information that has gone unmentioned about this episode by Bible scholars and theologians is the way these people perceived and engaged their reality. And it had to do with their thinking, speaking, and acting. All of us do it, but they did it in a different way—in a more advanced way. The apostle Paul tells us,

When I was a child, I spake as a child, I understood as a child, I thought as a child: but when I became a man, I put away childish things. (1 Corinthians 13:11)

- "I spoke as a child"—speaking.
- "I thought as a child"—thinking.
- "I put away childish things"—acting.

How does one take and use these faculties that everyone possesses to benefit us so that we may better serve the kingdom of God for the next season that the Lord is bringing us into? The answer is "future!" Yes! "Thinking future in the present tense!" You see, future in and of itself is in the clouds, and we know it to be in the heavenly places, but "future now," in the present tense, brings forth results. The future in the present tense is action based and result orientated. It's about solutions, innovation, and imagination. It's about taking action, "going for it," and doing something! The LORD said, "And this they begin to do." God is letting us know that there is power in using the future in the present tense to start something.

- "Lest we be scattered abroad"—thinking future.
- "Come, let us build us a city and a tower"—speaking future.
- "And this they begin to do"—acting future.

As they journeyed, they found a plain—a field. I think about it as a wide space, a canvas with the potential to be filled with some-thing—"whatever" and "anything"—unlimited! Then they dwelt there. Men and women are very resourceful and creative. It's in the nature of man to start creating and inventing things to make life more efficient and provide comfort.

"And they said one to another." They spoke; speech is very infec-tious. What did they speak? They spoke of the vision that most like-ly originated in the mind of one person. Before any word was loosed concerning that vision, it was first a thought that was formed and came out of the "imagination"—out of that beautiful word "*yetser!*" I can see a person under a tree or reclining upon a big stone, looking out into an empty plain, beholding everything that could be, as our Heavenly Father also did when He "beheld the earth, and, lo, it was without form, and void" (Jeremiah 4:23). They thought about it, spoke about it, and acted upon it! God had to put a halt to their building project. "Stop! Stop! You know too much!" And because they knew too much, they could thus "do too much."

"And this they begin to do: and now nothing will be restrained from them, which they have imagined to do." This wisdom was not wrong; what was wrong was that they were using it to defy the will of God. After the flood, they had been commanded to be fruitful, to multiply, and to fill the earth (Genesis 9:1).

Kingdom, "Let us begin to do." Let us apply what the Holy Spirit has taught us through the scriptures. So what will happen when the temple worldwide faces and prays to God with one accord in prayer and supplication? "He will answer us from heaven," as the Word says,

> And it shall come to pass in that day, I will hear, saith
> the LORD, I will hear the heavens, and they shall hear
> the earth; and the earth shall hear the corn, and the wine,
> and the oil; and they shall hear Jezreel. (Hosea 2:21–22)

And on "that day," when He answers, what shall become of "the little seed"?

> For the seed shall be prosperous; the vine shall give her
> fruit, and the ground shall give her increase, **and the
> heavens shall give their dew**; and I will cause the remnant of this people to possess all these things. (Zechariah 8:12, emphasis added)

The heavens will answer the earth; the heavens will give their dew (rain); the little seed will be prosperous; and the earth ("the people") will answer by giving her increase of grain, new wine, and oil (manifestation)!

We must remain connected and united, as the church, the body of Christ, and sons of the kingdom (children of God); as the little seeds; and as the Tabernacle of David.

Log on to **www.jessesplace.org** and share with us and the world what our Heavenly Father is doing in your life. Be a living witness to His power, working through your vision, the one that you have written, planted, or that is already in full fruition. If this book has inspired you in any way, we want to know about it. The vision is given to you for the profit of all. Also, be sure to make your Isaiah 64:1, **"Rend the Heavens,"** prayer on our website's blog. Thank you.

Jesus Christ loves you. I love you (and we at Jesse's Place Organization love you). Remember that we "can" and we, as a team, "shall bring down the heavens!" Amen.

In the meantime, "we shall continue in prayer and supplications, asking the Lord that He 'rend the heavens by sending down the latter rain of the Holy Spirit.'" We shall continue digging our ditches and preparing our barns so that He may say of us, in approval, "And this they begin to do, and now nothing will be withheld from them, which they have imagined to do. Well done, good and faithful servants. Enter into My rest!"

> Therefore be patient, brethren, until the coming of the Lord. See how the farmer waits for the precious fruit of the earth, waiting patiently for it until it receives the early and latter rain. You also be patient. Establish your hearts, for the coming of the Lord is at hand. (James 5:7–8 NKJV)

In closing, we are not the same sleeping Christians that we were in the beginning. We are awake and ready! The Holy Bible speaks about a valley of vision. Our valley of vision is where we began, and we treaded it together, line upon line, step upon step, precept upon precept. We also stood and together traversed the valley of dry bones, where we prophesied! We now stand yet upon another valley, and though we can walk through it together, the decision is to be made by you and you alone; it's a decision with eternal consequences. "Multitudes, multitudes in the valley of decision: for the day of the LORD is near in the valley of decision" (Joel 3:14).

My people, God through His Word, says,

> I call heaven and earth to record this day against you, that I have set before you life and death, blessing and cursing: therefore choose life, that both thou and thy seed may live. (Deuteronomy 30:19)

My brethren, right now, it's just you and God, and He further pleads,

> For He says: "In an acceptable time I have heard you, and in the day of salvation I have helped you." Behold, now is the accepted time; behold, now is the day of salvation. (2 Corinthians 6:2 NKJV)

How does one escape a sentence of everlasting hell? The Holy Bible tells us,

> That if thou shalt confess with thy mouth the Lord Jesus, and shalt believe in thine heart that God hath raised him from the dead, thou shalt be saved. For with the heart

man believeth unto righteousness; and with the mouth
confession is made unto salvation. (Romans 10:9–10)

If you just now believed, it means that you got saved by receiving
salvation through Jesus Christ, and I welcome you into the kingdom of
God. Now take up your cross, along with your vision, for the Christians
of today have places to evangelize, we have people to heal, and we have
visions to see! "Come to pass."

This is not the end; this is merely our new beginning.

And the Spirit and the bride say, "Come!" And let him
who hears say, "Come!" And let him who thirsts come.
Whoever desires, let him take the water of life freely.
(Revelation 22:17 NKJV)

Amen, Amen, and Amen!

THE VISION OF ONE ACCORD

Then the LORD answered me and said: "Write the vision and make it plain on tablets, that he may run who reads it."

—Habakkuk 2:2 NKJV

"If you know that the message contained within this book is true, then you have a moral and spiritual mandate, as well as a responsibility, to tell everyone you know about it, beginning with your home, neighbors, and community—'the nations.'

Run with it, my good runner!"

ABOUT THE AUTHOR

Jesse Suarez is a Mexican-American Christian man who, by the grace of God, was released after serving 14 1/2 years in prison. He diligently fought the appellate courts through the appeal process, and after numerous denials and resentencings, he finally received his freedom. During his incarceration, he married Sandra Suarez, a daughter of the Most High God, and they conceived Zoe-mama. Today, he is the co-founder of Jesse's Place Organization, which focuses on prison advocacy, prison ministry, and homeless street outreach. Prior to his release, he wrote the book *The Little Seed* as proof that God can use anybody regardless of their past mistakes. His life's purpose and mission are to serve the Kingdom of God by running with the vision all over the world, spreading the love, forgiveness, and power of Jesus Christ, so that the prisoners may be set FREE!

Made in United States
Troutdale, OR
05/22/2024

20062868R00146